Provoking Thought

For
John Dale
with admiration for your
status as one of the
largest donors in the
history of Juniata College

Leland Miles
10 /18/ 01

The public has no idea what goes on at a faculty meeting

Provoking Thought

What Colleges Should Do For Students

By

Leland Miles

PHOENIX PUBLISHING

West Kennebunk, Maine

The cartoon which embellishes the
jacket and appears as a frontispiece
was created by George Joseph,
of the
Louisville Courier-Journal

Cataloging-in-Publication Data

Miles, Leland.
    Provoking thought : what colleges should do for stu-
dents / by Leland Miles.
        p. cm.
    ISBN 0-914659-92-8
    1. Education, Higher—Aims and objectives. I. Title

LB2324 .M55 2000
378'.01—dc21   00-065251

Printed in the United States of America

To
the real-life cast of characters who people this book,
from the erudite to the unlearned,
from college presidents, trustees, and faculty
to parents, alumni, counselors, students,
and just plain Joes.
You will recognize yourselves in the pages that follow,
even when you are not named.

Contents

Acknowledgments

T HIS BOOK COULD not have been written without the help of many college leaders, professors, counselors, alumni, parents, editors, and general readers, together with students of all ages, types, and vocations, who took the time to critique an early version of this work. Especially must I pay tribute to those kind but candid people who some years ago comprised the "Making of a Book" seminar at New College, Sarasota. For many weeks, these early readers were my instructors, and I their pupil. In its final form, the style, structure, and subject matter of *Provoking Thought* reflects the advice and sometimes the emotional pleas of those seminar members—even to the extent of including chapters on love and friendship.

Two people deserve special commendation. Katherine Zadrovicz, my former assistant, struggled patiently through the typing and editing of earlier versions of this work. And Professor George Blake gave brave advice, which turned this work into something far more significant than originally intended. I am also indebted to Kathleen Ober, my assistant during the six years (1991-97) that I represented the International Association of University Presidents at the United Nations. She not only typed the final version of *Provoking Thought*, but along the way made valuable suggestions for improvement both in style and substance. In particular, her challenging of certain ideas forced me to reassure myself that I really meant everything I was saying. She represents the kind of graduate that I wish every college could produce.

L.M.

Fairfield, Connecticut
February 2001

Provoking Thought

Prologue

WHILE IN FLORIDA not long ago, I was looking for a Christmas gift for a scientist friend. I lean toward books for gifts, because where else can you get something for $30 that lasts more than two or three years? My friend is interested in ideas, works at a college, and loves to laugh.

So I went into Charlie's, a large and (despite the name) fairly sophisticated bookstore in downtown Sarasota, and talked to the manager. "Do you have a humorous book here dealing with college as an adventure in ideas?" I asked. Hearing no response, I added, "As, you know, a preparation for the 21st Century." Looking incredulous, the manager blurted that he "never heard of" such a book. Shaking his head, he led me to some racks labeled "Study," where he pointed out the omnipresent guidebooks to colleges, and manuals on everything from getting through nursing exams to qualifying for the FBI. The prize was a volume entitled *College 101-Making the Most of the Freshman Year,* which on examination treated everything *except* the intellectual side of college life.

At several other Sarasota bookstores, I got the same response. At my request, a colleague checked out Rizzoli, Dalton, Barnes & Noble, and Doubleday bookstores in New York, without success. Finally I wound up at Kingsley's Book Store on elegant St. Armand's Circle, across the causeway from Sarasota. Here, again I repeated my request for a humorous book dealing with college as an adventure in ideas. The woman clerk whom I addressed drew a blank, and the male clerk, whom she summoned and briefed, simply grimaced and said, "Wow! Tough!" A search of the total book store then ensued, as both clerks, with me in tow, rummaged furiously through the racks on humor, education, psychology, and so on. Unsuccessful in their pursuit, both employees disappeared into a rear office for a whispered conference with the manager. He finally emerged with a show of irritation and exclaimed, "We can't help you. Why don't *you* write such a book?" So I did. And here it is.

In *Provoking Thought* I seek to comment on the past, present, and future of college education in the United States, based on my own half century of sometimes humorous experiences as student, professor, scholar, dean, president, and board chair at many types of institutions: new and old, small and large, public and private, famous and otherwise. Along the way, through luck rather than any particular merit, I was involved in many of the major developments, crises, and upheavals that have affected college education since World War II.

In the late 1940's, "GI Bill" veterans flooded campuses and brought a new sense of urgency to learning. A decade later, strictly liberal arts colleges began to add "practical" programs. The 1960's saw student unrest, which disrupted some campuses, but raised legitimate public policy issues. Collective bargaining stormed into higher education in the '70's; international and interdisciplinary movements emerged in the '80's; and political correctness raised its controversial head in the most recent decade. During these fifty years, for many social and economic reasons, part-time (usually older) students emerged as an important part of educational demographics; Continuing Education programs began to re-ignite retirees and adults who had never finished their degrees; and community colleges came into their own, as a respected and often innovative transition to upper-class college study. I was there when these events occurred, initially as an observer and sideline participant, and later as a so-called "major player."

Anyone who has lived through these experiences over such a long period of time is entitled to express an opinion on what colleges should do for students, and therefore on what a college education really is, or should be, especially as we enter the 21st Century. In the chapters that follow, I identify the qualities that colleges should develop in their graduates and explain why those qualities are important, how they relate to my own life, and why they are necessary if we wish to achieve fulfillment in work and play.

In this book, the reader will not find footnotes, bibliography, or other scholarly paraphernalia in defense of my views. The evidence supporting my conclusions is nothing more or less than my fifty years of experiences in higher education—experiences that I cheerfully share in the pages that follow. These experiences cover all levels and types of higher education, from Freshman English to Ph.D. studies, from nursing schools to chiropractic and nutrition programs, from evening school to technology research centers.

However, my heart has always been with full-time undergraduate education, which still includes a significant part of the college population, and which still provides half or more of the revenue supporting American undergraduate colleges. *Provoking Thought* focuses on such education, not because it is "better" than any other level or type, but because it is the field I know best, and can speak to with the greatest conviction. Moreover, many of the human qualities that full-time undergraduate study can produce are also achievable through part-time and even graduate education.

My near certainty today on these matters stands in amusing contrast to my ambivalence more than a half century ago, when I began my odyssey through the world of higher education. Even though I was student president when I graduated from Forest Park High School in Baltimore in 1941, I had no idea where to go for a "college education," or even what a college was supposed to do once I got there. Neither of my parents was a college graduate, so they had no idea either. My father thought it would be great if I went to the Naval Academy, my mother was amenable to almost any honest career, and I was at a complete loss as to what I should be, or do. For me at that stage, college was a kind of romantic limbo, a sort of Spenserian bower of bliss. Through it I could extend the carefree life of high school for four more years, put off any important decisions to "later," and continue to think about the future rather than actually entering it.

At this point, Providence stepped in. Shortly after I received my high school diploma, an "a cappella" choir from Juniata College in Huntingdon, Pennsylvania, sang at my church in Baltimore. They seemed to sing well, even without musical accompaniment. I assumed that the college was too poor to afford a piano player, or that the church had failed to provide one. It was only later I learned that "a cappella" means "with voices only" and that the Juniata choir excelled at that type of singing.

My mother introduced me to the choir director. After hearing me sing a few bars, he diplomatically suggested that my strengths were probably not in music. But, he said, Juniata could provide jobs in public information and theater if I chose to enroll. He emphasized that such jobs would largely cover the $600 per year tuition/room/board fees, a significant figure to many families in those days. So I became the first Episcopalian ever to attend this Church of the Brethren College. Considered an oddity, I was constantly asked to read from the Episcopal Prayer Book at the required chapel services. Thinking my new Brethren friends equally odd, I constantly challenged their argument that dancing was morally evil, a position which got me into trouble more than once on that devout campus.

Obviously, college life has changed since 1941. Annual tuition and room and board figures have soared to five digits, and required chapel has disappeared along with many other requirements. "Touch dancing" (as the students now call it) is making a comeback, but rock is still in the saddle, and people like me consider ear plugs vital equipment when attending a student dance. What has changed even more is the orientation to college life.

When I was a high school graduate, there were few books available telling you how to get into college, and how to "make it" once there. Today there are hundreds of such books, mostly manuals and guides, which tell the would-be freshman how to select and rate a college, how to "crack" the SAT's, how to handle an admissions interview, how and where to find financial aid, how to prepare for freshman orientation week, how to adjust to dormitory life, how to fool your professors into giving you good grades, how to get through the allegedly inevitable "sophomore slump," how to keep from getting too much distracted by football games, beer blasts, and fraternity parties, and how as a senior ultimately to achieve (as one book puts it) "happiness, popularity, and success."

To a large extent, these manuals and guides deal with the mechanics of getting in and through college and with the freshman's psychological and sociological adjustment once admitted. Reading the best of these works might help the would-be freshman to study better, improve vocabulary, exercise his rights, discover learning disabilities, avoid drugs, transcend gender problems, maintain mental health, and develop self-confidence.

Most such books are commendable and worthwhile, but they are not at the center of getting and later using a college education. The central purpose of going to college is not to play soccer, win the lead role in a play, find a compatible roommate, join a sorority or fraternity, get straight "A's", or find a spouse. These things may contribute toward the desired end. But the central purpose of college is to develop an initial competence in one's chosen field of endeavor, and *simultaneously* to expand one's intellectual horizons, to plunge into the adventure of ideas, to live for a few precious years the exciting life of the mind— and in the process to begin to imagine the hopes and problems that lie beyond 2000 A.D. The central purpose is to learn, as Cardinal Newman said, to value knowledge not only for its practical applications, but also for its capacity to enrich the mind and increase the joy of living.

None of this means that earlier educational efforts are less important. A young woman sitting with me on a plane once asked what I did for a living. I told her, and she replied, "I'm *just* an elementary school teacher." The word "just" should never be used in referring to pre-college education. It is in these earlier stages that teachers are asked to build our children, in the same way that workers build our homes. At their best, elementary and secondary schools construct the mental sets that are pre-requisites to satisfactory college work. College professors can then build on the foundation constructed by their predecessors.

Florence Lane, my math teacher at Forest Park, was such a "predecessor" for me. She could smell bubble gum at ten yards, even if you hid it under your tongue, but for me she had one redeeming quality. Thanks to her, I was well grounded in algebra when I enrolled at Juniata. Likewise, Margaret Hufnagle revealed to me the hidden structure of English, Genevieve Butler inspired me to love semi-classical music, and Vernon Vavrina taught me kindness as well as French. But it was from Miss Emily, the principal of Windsor Hills Elementary School, that I learned my most important lesson, that consequence follows cause. Caught by Miss Waskins as I lit a match in class (she could smell sulfur like Miss Lane could smell gum), I was dragged before Miss Emily, whose office doubled as guillotine. Glaring across her vast mahogany desk, she looked like a squatting bulldog. I was summarily expelled, and told to return with my mother the next morning. To delay the inevitable, I climbed a tree, sulked over Miss Waskin's betrayal, and tried to figure out how to tell Mom while keeping Dad in the dark.

This book is for all those, regardless of age or vocation, who care about learning—who recognize its potential to open minds, lift the spirit, and catapult us into a dazzling new era of ideas and achievements. Better to inspire minds to open, than denounce them for being closed. In recent years we have seen many books which speak cynically of higher education. Such works, critics claim, are signals that America's love affair with colleges is over. Maybe so, but not according to this work. Given inspired faculty, sympathetic counseling, and an educational philosophy relevant to the new century, college students can have an even more exciting adventure than I experienced many years ago.

A case in point is William Phillips, a member of the Juniata class of 1970. On October 15, 1997, at 3:00 A.M., he received a wake-up call from Stockholm. He had won the Nobel Prize in physics! "With that phone call," reported the *Washington Post,* "a blaze of glory and a bunch of money fell into the life of a hitherto anonymous government scientist." A few days later, in an interview with the *Altoona Mirror,* Dr. Phillips drew attention to the debt he owed his alma mater. "I learned a lot of intangibles there," he said. "I learned about growing up and becoming a complete individual. Juniata . . . produces . . . good scientists, but it also produces good people."

Bill Phillips' theme is also the theme of this book. In the chapters that follow, I suggest that the aim of a college education should be to teach us not just how to earn a living, but also how to live, and that the qualities derived from that kind of education can enhance our performance in both spheres. I try to focus on one such quality in each chapter, moving from relatively simple ideas to more complex ones, much like a freshman evolves gradually into a senior. In the Epilogue, these ideas and qualities are then merged into a mosaic of the kind of leader needed for the 21st Century. As I proceed in this manner, I hope to persuade the reader that the humanities, as broadly defined, are as much needed as technology as we enter the New Millennium.

1

College Versus Education

"Mr. Sikorsky, should I go to college?"

WHILE I WAS PRESIDENT at Alfred University in upstate New York, a noted politician from Hawaii enrolled his daughter in the nursing program. The problem was that his daughter did not want to be a nurse. She was a licensed pilot, loved everything about aircraft, and hoped to become a maintenance crew chief for a major airline. She obviously belonged at an aeronautical institute, and that is where she decided to go.

When the father got wind of the situation, he hastily flew across the Pacific, came to my office, and implored me to persuade his daughter to stay put. But I was on her side. As I learned from conversing with her father, to him college was first and foremost a status symbol, a colored seal to stick on the rear window of the family car. "A mechanic!" he groaned. "How will I explain this to friends?" This attitude, shared by many parents, goes a long way toward explaining the decline in esteem for the crafts and trades in America, even though such vocations are not only honorable, but critical to a functioning society.

A 1997 issue of the *Connecticut Post* carries the headline, "Industries Threatened as Student Base Dwindles." The gist of the story is that manufacturing desperately needs skilled labor, yet enrollment in technical-vocational schools has dropped by half in ten years. The major obstacle blocking students from industry, we are told, is parents. They keep saying over and over, "We want our children to go to college."

But college is not for everybody. It definitely is not for young people whose temperament, interests, and life goals are out of sync with the requirements for a bachelor's degree. As we learn from the case of the Hawaiian politician, parents are engaged in a futile enterprise when they try to impose a traditional education on reluctant offspring. Even if sons and daughters go willingly to college, the results may not be what they and their parents anticipated. The terms "college" and "education" do not necessarily go together—some people with college diplomas are not educated, and vice versa.

My mother is an example of the vice versa. "Marie Fitz" (as she was called) never had the family resources to go to college, and financial aid was rare in those days. Yet she became director of one of the largest Red Cross chapters in the country, was well read in biography, and an authority on English history. After I received my Ph.D. from Chapel Hill, she gave a reception in my honor, and proudly invited her friends to "show me off." "Who was the greatest figure in the Renaissance?" asked a woman guest, upon discovering my major interest. "Oh, that's easy," I replied knowingly. "Leonardo Da Vinci. After all, he's the one who claimed all knowledge for his province." There were murmurs of admiration from my appreciative audience. But at that heady moment, my mother interrupted. "I don't think Da Vinci made that claim, darling. I believe it was Francis Bacon, during Elizabeth's reign in England."

Was I annoyed! My admiring audience was now frowning and asking the silent question, "Does he know what he is talking about?" When the last guest left, Marie Fitz and I rushed for the encyclopedia. Of course, she was right. In some ways, that was the beginning of *my* education.

My thinking on college versus education was further clarified some years later when my wife, Ginny, and I were en route from Honduras to New York. We were the only passengers on board the *Metapan*, a freighter hauling bananas for United Fruit. It was a weather-beaten ship, and the captain, Ezra Boyle, was a bit worse for wear himself. He was a ferocious looking fellow, with darting black eyes, a huge hawk nose, and a frightening scowl. We learned later that he had only a sixth grade education, a fact that would have endeared him to my mother.

On the second day from port, I was on the fantail of the ship when Boyle came up beside me and rested his arms on the rail. He was wearing a wrinkled khaki uniform with no insignia. We began to talk, and suddenly, I don't know how, we were on the subject of wisdom. Off-handedly I said, "You know, Captain, Plato said that a wise man is a man who knows that he knows not.".

Immediately I was embarrassed at having put him at a disadvantage with my superior knowledge. But to my amazement, he shot back, "I know, Doctor. Plato also said . . ." and in an instant he gave me two more quotes from the same Platonic dialogue! If the railing had been less firm, I would have fallen overboard.

With that verbal exchange to establish his intellectual equality, Captain Boyle took me to his quarters, and I found myself gaping at a substantial library mounted on floor-to-ceiling shelves. He had all the classics—the Greek playwrights, the Norse epics, the works of Shakespeare, Milton, Dickens, on and on. He had read them all. He explained in a somewhat embarrassed manner that once he got the ship into deep water, there was little to do until he guided it into the next port. So for twenty years, on a nondescript freighter, he had read and lived among the world's great thinkers, becoming in the process more educated than most college graduates ever are.

In a way, Boyle was like Mabel Dunham. For several years I moderated "Casing the Classics" over CBS-TV in Louisville. One week I was doing Ralph Waldo Emerson's essay "Self Reliance," and invited a Unitarian clergyman as one of the guests. In searching for a contrasting panelist, I learned of Mabel, a dowdy, middle-aged lady who worked as a foreman in a shoe factory. She had no formal education, but was reputed to have developed a fantastic knowledge of Emerson's works and his philosophy of transcendentalism. In reviewing her background, I found she had assembled a library as impressive as Boyle's, containing every book ever written by or about Emerson. Despite this, my TV director and crew objected strenuously to bringing her on the show. They felt that she, an uneducated working-class person, would be no match for the erudite clergyman with his Doctor of Divinity degree. "She'll be humiliated," they protested, "and the situation will be embarrassing for everyone."

I invited her anyway, and my colleagues were right. The situation was indeed embarrassing—for the clergyman. He had miscalculated his opponent and came unprepared. She did not need to prepare. She was far beyond him in a knowledge of Emerson, even outclassing him in a discussion of the "Divinity School Address." The Doctor of Divinity never spoke to me again, but Mabel and I became good friends.

Ezra Boyle and Mabel Dunham embody my idea of what education is all about. Both became competent managers, in their cases through on-the-job training: Boyle as a ship captain, and Mabel as a factory foreman. Yet both moved beyond their occupations and livelihood to deepen their understanding of the world through intellectual endeavor. If people can educate themselves in this manner, why should anyone go to college? Why put up with the admission jitters, financial aid anxieties, final exam traumas? The answer is that college, with all its flaws, has certain advantages over going it alone. Thousands of students graduate from colleges every year. But comparable self-education, wholly outside the university setting, is achieved, if at all, only by extreme sacrifice over a long period of time, and only by overcoming obstacles formidable enough to daunt the spirit of all but the most stout-hearted.

To be sure, these obstacles have been diminished by the Internet, on-line courses, distance learning, and especially interactive television. This latter brings the student and the professor "face to face" in a virtual classroom where the one can question and the other can answer and explain. Imagine the delight that Ezra Boyd and Mabel Dunham would have felt had they been given the opportunities provided by such technology.

Even with such opportunities, however, the self-educated lack the freedom of the full-time undergraduate. People like Boyle and Dunham have demanding jobs and/or family responsibilities. When they end work at dark, they may be too weary from the day's labor, or too distracted by domestic problems, to focus on their chosen fields of study. In addition, there is no freshman orientation to teach study skills, no introductory courses to enforce academic discipline. Thanks to Andrew Carnegie, there might be a good public library close enough to profit from, but aspirants to self-education will have, *really* face-to-face, no college faculty to engage them in back-and-forth discussion, no counselors to smooth the way, and no classrooms or resident halls in which to debate ideas with their peers over a significant period of time.

Much of education comes from the electric sparks that fly from the clash of good minds. In an intellectual sense, Captain Boyle had no one to "clash" with on his freighter, nor did Mabel Dunham in her shoe factory. Neither could rap with a roommate from a different socioeconomic status, ethnic background, or religious belief. Nor could either step across the street from their residence halls to the arts center, as Sarasota's New College students can, to watch Sophocles' *Medea* performed by the noted Asolo Players, or hear a Palestinian woman lecture on her version of West Bank problems.

The result is that most self-education is understandably warped and erratic. Apart from their management skills, Boyle's and Dunham's knowledge was limited to particular areas of the humanities. Their learning, extraordinary as it was, lacked the sweep and scope of a broad education, which requires studies in all disciplines (including the sciences) under a formalized guidance program. And finally, after all the efforts these two made to educate themselves, neither had any credentials to show for it, no certification that they were, by reason of their expanded knowledge, qualified for a higher position. Like it or not, credentials of some kind are mandatory in almost every profession today.

Between college education with its credentials, and self-education with its sacrifice, lies a middle way, that of pursuing a college education part-time. Almost half of all undergraduates today are 25 or older and most of them are now taking this middle way. They include working people returning to complete their degrees, and retirees attending on a non-credit basis to recharge their mental batteries. My friend, Bill Paul, is a prime example of these non-traditional students.

Bill began his career as a machinist at the Sikorsky Aircraft factory. One day the company president, Igor Sikorsky, toured the factory floor. When Bill's turn came to shake hands with the father of the helicopter, he said, "Mr. Sikorsky, my name is William S. Paul. Should I go to college?" "Of course," replied the great man. "What should I major in?" Bill persisted. "Mechanical engineering," snapped Igor, who never wasted much time in making decisions. And so Bill Paul went to the University of Bridgeport in Connecticut on a part-time basis for seven years to earn his engineering degree. As time went on, he rose through the ranks to become president of the company that Sikorsky had founded. One day William S. Paul was himself touring the factory floor, in emulation of his noted mentor. A young machinist approached him boldly and said, "Mr. Paul, my name is Joseph W. Sykes. Should I go to college?" Bill stared at him suspiciously for a long moment, then said with a grin, "Hey Joe, you're after my job, aren't you!"

Over the years, driving home from campus each evening, I have seen hundreds of Bill Pauls trudging toward classrooms, determined to earn degrees despite jobs and family obligations. Many of these students I remember still: the wife who missed her husband so much, she joined him in law school and earned her degree at the same time; the blind student whose devoted girlfriend guided him over the years to an Education diploma; the 67-year-old Puerto Rican woman who, when asked to stand and receive the plaudits for finally earning her bachelor's degree in nursing, leaped up and clasped her hands over her head in a boxer's victory salute. These are among the real heroes and heroines of education. My admiration for them also applies to many self-taught adults and full-time undergraduates, who in their own right but in different ways become equally valuable to America.

All avenues to education, whether self-taught, campus-oriented, or part-time, have two things in common: there are no guaranteed results, and all require dedication and discipline. To be sure, the full-time resident choice is most efficient, providing the stimulating support of other good minds, the convenience of accessible libraries, state-of-the-art computers, programs and laboratory equipment, and professional guidance in a chosen field of study pursued over three or four consecutive years. But even with these advantages, the student must ultimately depend upon his or her own resources to "make it," not only by achieving competency in a chosen field, but also by developing an understanding of other fields of endeavor. Attaining these two goals is a tall order, and many freshmen are certain to fail somewhere along the way.

2

Learning from Failing

"Dear Mom and Dad, there's also been a problem with the Volvo."

I N HIS BOOK *Living With High Risk Technology,* Yale sociologist Charles Perrow suggests that in the New Millennium, learning from failing will be more needed because failing will be more frequent. As technology becomes more prevalent and more complex, we will become less able to operate our machinery, no matter how well we have been trained or how many safety devices have been installed. Some technology already moves faster than the mind can think, so human errors are already multiplying at a disconcerting rate. Those in the 21st Century who cannot learn quickly from errors and adjust promptly for them may find themselves facing disasters larger and more dangerous than the crises of the outgoing century—Bhopal, Challenger, Chernobyl, Exxon Valdez, and Valujet.

Given this scenario, it behooves higher education to place more emphasis on the process of learning by failing. Unfortunately, most colleges have a limited tolerance for failure. Students who fail a few courses struggle under an administrative cloud of inferiority, and are often avoided by fellow students who want to escape guilt by association. Ilene Rosenstein, counseling director at the University of Pennsylvania, notes that today's college students are busy and schedule driven, but many of them, lacking guidance, "have not learned how to deal with failure." The same applies to many pre-college students. A much admired New College senior once confessed to me that he was so afraid of failure that he almost decided against college. Many high school grads, he said, move right to the brink of going to college, and then retreat because they fear they "don't have the brains."

Interestingly, neither Thomas Edison nor Winston Churchill "had the brains" by academic measures. A principal told Edison's mother not to send him to high school, because he would never make it. So young Thomas puttered around the basement, produced the first incandescent light bulb, and changed applied physics forever. Churchill's academic performance at his prep school, Harrow, was mediocre, and his general conduct, as described by the headmaster, was "disgraceful." Worse, he failed twice before being admitted to Sandhurst, the British military academy. But young Winston struggled on, eventually helping to save the free world.

It might be that brains are overrated. Most of us are blessed with an adequate amount of intelligence. What is really needed and more rare in any line of endeavor is perseverance. When my son Greg graduated from Loomis, he selected a quotation from Franklin Roosevelt to place under his yearbook photo. It read, "Tell me why the marsh is impossible to cross, and I will tell you why I can cross it if I try." It is this kind of attitude that colleges should promote in their admission booklets, orientation programs, and counseling sessions.

Some years ago Alfred, inspired by an earlier program at Boston University, inaugurated an experiment called "Double O," for Operation Opportunity. Each year, forty students were admitted who, judged by conventional standards of test scores and class standing, were incapable of doing college work. In each case their only recommendation was a letter from their principal or headmaster, stating in essence that despite a dismal record, they had hidden abilities, special qualities like perseverance, or special situations like broken homes, that justified their being given a last chance. In the early semesters, "Double O" students were assigned lighter class loads and more counseling than their classmates. Their performance was generally wobbly and faltering for the first two years. Some failed, all struggled. But by their senior year, many of them were doing as well as their fellows, and some even out-performed regular students. One "Double O" member became student president, and another the editor of the student newspaper.

"Double O" would seem to prove that perseverance, combined with reasonable intelligence, pays off. But with all the perseverance in the world, few students will graduate from college without being defeated by something. They will fail an exam, be passed over for captain of the hockey team, lose a student officer election, not be named to the collegiate *Who's Who*. Older, part-time students may fail to adjust to the burden of required reading, to the presence of young people in the classroom, or to the theoretical tendencies of professors who don't live in the "real world." Colleges should emphasize in their publications that experimenting is applauded, reasonable risks are admirable, failure can be positive, and college a safe place to learn from failing. At the University of Houston, Professor Jack Matson teaches a course affectionately known as "Failure 101." The main requirement of this course, officially named "Innovative Design for Civil Engineers," is to deliberately create a device or machine *that does not work*. As Matson sees it, failure is the other side of success. Only when we have built something that does not work, can we understand what will.

Seen rightly, college represents young peoples' last chance to make major mistakes with only minor penalties. One can select the wrong friends and not be sued, fall in love with the wrong person and not get divorced, choose the wrong major and not get fired, embrace a variant philosophy and not be ridiculed, give a wrong answer and not be investigated by a Congressional committee. The lessons learned from these debacles become priceless after college, when we all fail more than we succeed. Critic John Ciardi once said that a good poet writes bad poems nine out of ten times. As a minor poet, I would settle for that average any time.

Frankly, colleges should encourage students to fail and recover, rather than to perform brilliantly and then fall hard when they sometimes do. Maybe I feel strongly about this because of my own experiences. During World War II, would-be navigators like me had to qualify as aerial gunners before they could go to advanced navigation school. So I was sent to Panama City in Florida for gunnery training. It was a discomforting experience, since I had never owned a gun except a BB rifle, and I discarded that after unintentionally hitting a bird. My aim was so bad that the safest place to stand, when I was shooting, was directly in front of the target. When grades were posted, I was near the bottom of the class.

Luckily for me, my roommate was a college math major from Macalester College in Minnesota. The final test consisted of shooting from a truck-mounted turret at a target towed across the line of sight. My friend agreed to calculate the theoretical "lead" necessary to hit the target consistently. The "lead" turned out to be forty feet, which seemed way off. But what could I lose? So I kept my gunsight forty feet in front of the moving target, pressed the trigger, and hoped my orange-colored bullets would do the rest. When the target was inspected, it was full of orange holes. "Who had the orange bullets?' barked the instructor. "I did, sir," I replied. "You? Miles? Good God!" At first I was accused of cheating, but they had to accept the evidence—Miles had orange bullets, there were orange holes in the target, what could they do?

These experiences were much in my mind later, when Alfred's ROTC wanted to establish an award in my name. The Professor of Military Science asked whether I wanted the award to be for the "best cadet of the year," or for the cadet with the "most improved performance." Remembering my experiences in training, I said, "If it's all the same to you, Colonel, let's give it for the most improved performance. I can identify with that type better than the other." He smiled and said, "I understand." Perhaps he'd made mistakes too?

In helping students deal with mistakes and failures, colleges should stress the need for perspective. One night in New York I encountered a gentleman slowly rotating around a lamppost, pushing hard against it every few inches. As he circled the post, pushing here and there, he look increasingly troubled. When he got all the way round to where he started, he stopped, shook his head in disbelief, and muttered, "My God. Walled in!" Like the inebriated New Yorker, all of us get "walled in" from time to time. But with perspective, failures can often be blessings in disguise. When King Henry threw Thomas More into prison, More discovered that his new status was a blessing. Why? Because it gave him a chance to think, undistracted by material possessions and the outside world.

As More learned, what seems disastrous today is often comforting or even amusing tomorrow. My failure to make the varsity ice hockey team in high school caused me untold anguish at the time. I had spent my entire summer working to earn a pair of Canadian skates, and had practiced diligently, in private as well as with the team. When the final roster was posted and my name was not on it, I reacted with hurt and anger. I read the list over and over, unable to believe my name wasn't there. The coach was obviously stupid, I thought. He couldn't recognize talent when he saw it. But I survived. In fact, the experience forced me to realize that I was not a talented athlete, and that nobody can be good at everything.

Students not only need to develop a sense of perspective for themselves, but their parents and spouses need to do so too. At mid-term a few years ago, Cornell University sophomore Sherry Addison wrote a letter to her parents which read, "Dear Mom and Dad, I've encountered a few problems in the past week. First, there was a fire in the dorm, started by my smoking in bed. The mattress caught fire and the new fall wardrobe you bought me burned up. There's also been a problem with the Volvo. A tree got in the way and I totaled the car." As if this litany of woes was not sufficient, Sherry then added a final paragraph: "Mom and Dad, I think the president here has gone crazy. He's ordered a tuition surcharge, which means I'll need an additional $1500, over and above the cost of replacing the car and the clothing. Love, Sherry." At the bottom of the letter she wrote a P.S.: "Please see reverse side." The trembling parents turned the sheet over and read the following short note: "Nothing I said on the other side of this letter really happened. What really *did* happen was that I got a "D" in Psychology, and I wanted you to keep it in perspective."

As Professor Matson would say, the other side of failure is, of course, success. Parents are especially fond of this word. They understandably want their children to be "successful." But what do they mean—monetary success, a big house, luxury cars, a swimming pool? Some people who live in big houses are bores, or worse, tragedies. Some who drive luxury cars are pompous, shallow, mean, selfish. Some who have amassed fortunes are failures as parents, neighbors, people. Christopher Lasch, in his last collection of essays, argues that too many Americans are obsessed with "making it," and therefore ceaselessly "transfer luxuries into necessities." College is where students can think through for themselves the meaning of "success." The word might have more to do with character, competence, and community service than with status, salary and fame. Why are these distinctions not emphasized more frequently in college catalogues?

Many great figures were not successful by conventional standards. Albert Schweitzer gave up everything he was admired for—theology, the organ, teaching—to start a controversial hospital in Africa. For him success meant helping others, not boosting his reputation. For Robert

Browning, success meant striving, not achieving. "A man's reach should exceed his grasp," he wrote, "else what's a heaven for?" Ralph Abernathy, the great civil rights leader, asked that his epitaph read simply, "He tried."

One part of success is certainly the achievement of competence in one's chosen field. The irony here is that two-thirds of all freshmen don't know what they want to do. To which I say, so what? What's the rush? If a freshman approached me for career advice, I'd ask, "Why not wait a while? You think you might want to be a diplomat? Fine. A cinematographer? Great. A bio-medical engineer? Why not? But let's think about it." As Hemingway said in *The Old Man and the Sea*, for all of us there is a great fish out there somewhere. But we can't expect he will surface next to the boat. If we want to hook him, we must search for him. And the search will take time. It might take more time than the first two college years.

In *Walden*, Henry David Thoreau urged us to put foundations under our dreams. Colleges exist to help students follow that advice. But the first step for both students and counselors is to determine which dreams are realistic for the students involved. Do they have the temperament and capacity to be diplomats, or cinematographers, or whatever? Do they understand the academic preparation and hands-on experience necessary to achieve such a goal? Are they aware of the pressures, risks, and other negatives of such professions?

Unfortunately, this crucial process of career counseling is often disrupted by parents who have already pre-judged what their offspring should do. The painter, Paul Gauguin, began as a bank teller; the flutist, Pierre Rampaul, as a pre-med student; and the novelist, Kurt Vonnegut, as a public relations officer for General Electric. Like the story of the Hawaiian politician in Chapter 1, such switches are often the result of misguided parental attempts to impose careers upon their children. One of my best high school friends, Stephen Senning, wanted to be in the shipping business. He made ship models and talked about ships all the time. But his parents were adamant that he become a doctor, and he obliged. When they died, however, he immediately left his practice and returned to Grace Passenger Line in Baltimore, where he had worked as a teenager and gained his first love of the sea.

Just as Steve Senning got trapped in medicine, Robert Manry got trapped in journalism. Though a copy editor for the *Cleveland Plain*

Dealer, Manry had dreamed all his life of sailing the Atlantic in a home-made boat, as a prelude to a career on the sea. He finally built the boat—so small he named it *Tinkerbelle* after the tiny fairy in *Peter Pan*. The first time he tested the craft, he capsized it, because he had never sailed before. But he kept on practicing. People ridiculed him, his wife divorced him, his parents disowned him, the *Plain Dealer* fired him, the neighbors said he was a nut. But he got in his boat and crossed the Atlantic anyway. It took him eighty-seven days. He was washed overboard eight times.

When he reached Land's End off the coast of Britain, word went out that "the nut" might make it. So the owner of the *Plain Dealer* promptly flew to England, hired a motor launch, and came alongside *Tinkerbelle*, bobbing around Land's End. He offered Manry his job back. Manry told the owner what he could do with the *Plain Dealer*—and with the motor launch. Here was a dreamer who not only put a foundation under his dreams, but who risked failure and ridicule rather than back away from a goal he had carefully defined and prepared for. Senning and Manry shared similar goals. Unfortunately, each wasted half a life before grasping his dream. Colleges should be able to do better for the students under their care. Over half a century, I have watched, prodded, and cajoled hundreds of freshman and their parents. From that experience I draw a simple conclusion: Rushing to judgment on a career choice is foolish. But waiting too long can greatly diminish the opportunity to contribute to one's chosen field.

3

Mastering the Basics

"I'm at the bottom of things, lady. I made the whole thing tick."

FROM MY VARIOUS educational roles over the years, I have learned one common truth, namely, that the best defense against failure, and the best formula for success, is mastering the basics. Any one basic might appear trivial. But ignore it, and the damage is disproportionate to the error.

In the first chapter, I praised the learning of Ezra Boyle, captain of the *Metapan*. Boyle or someone like him must have been the inspiration for the story of the freighter captain who kept a key on a string around his neck. Whenever his ship approached a harbor entrance, he was observed to retire to his cabin, unlock his desk drawer, and peer in for five minutes or so. He would then re-lock the drawer, leave the cabin with new self-assurance, and proceed to command brilliantly as he shepherded his vessel in and out of port. There was of course intense speculation among the crew as to what was in the desk. When the captain died, the crew tore the key off his neck, rushed to his cabin, and unlocked the drawer. To their amazement, there was nothing there except a 3x5 card, on which was scrawled an instruction. It was difficult to read, because two key words had been crossed out and corrected. As corrected, the instruction read, "Starboard is *right* and port is *left*."

It is a good story, because it illustrates an important point: all professions, trades, and crafts, no matter how complex, depend upon a few basic principles. These "basics" must not only be learned at the outset; they must be rehearsed and reviewed again and again. No wonder airline pilots are required to review take-off procedures before every flight, and do so without the slightest hesitation.

No one can be competent in a field without mastering certain basic principles, whether the field is flying, chemistry, computer programming, or art. That is why the first two years of college are largely devoted to learning basic skills. Introductory "survey" and "foundation" courses lead to majors in the field. Although colleges always declare that the basics are important, such courses are often shunned by senior professors, who regard them as demeaning intrusions on their writing and research. Thus the 101-102 courses, as they are usually numbered, are often relegated to graduate assistants, or, on the smaller campus, to newly hired instructors with untenured status. The time has long since passed for colleges to put their practices where their rhetoric is. If basic courses are really important, only the most experienced and innovative faculty should be assigned to teach them, and such faculty should be promoted and recompensed at the same level as publishing scholars. One student grounded in the fundamentals and prepared to be a competent professional is worth at least as much as the typical research paper read by scholars at "learned society" meetings.

In the field of education, some of the fiercest proponents of the basics are athletic coaches. One day I was watching Alex Yunevitch, then the senior football coach in America, during practice at Alfred University. A halfback broke off tackle, dodged the linebackers, outran the safety, and raced sixty yards for a touchdown. The young man trotted back, smiling, expecting to be congratulated. Instead Alex glared at him and growled, "You carried the ball in the wrong hand."

J.M.W. Turner, one of the greatest English landscape painters, gradually moved from realism to more abstract works. But such an evolution would never have been possible had he not first mastered basic draftsmanship. Before surrealist Salvador Dali could paint a grotesque face or arm, he had to learn to draw a real one. We all must develop from a base. When we deviate, we must know what we are deviating from. The pianist, Victor Borge, is a master comedian precisely because his parodies are grounded in a solid knowledge of classical music and operatic history.

All of us at times seek to circumvent the basics, viewing them as an insult to our intelligence, or an unnecessary drag on getting the job done. Attempted shortcuts to knowledge, and to the basics that are a prelude to knowledge, can turn out to be time-consuming at best and even dangerous at worst. A case in point is Nathaniel Hawthorne's "Celestial Railroad." In this little-known classic, the author dreams he takes a trip over the same route traveled two centuries earlier by the title character in John Bunyan's *Pilgrim's Progress*. In that work, you will recall that the pilgrim had encountered a formidable array of obstacles in his efforts to travel from the City of Destruction to the Celestial City, which for Bunyan symbolized heaven.

But Hawthorne, re-tracing the path of that trip, discovers that everything has been streamlined. It is no longer necessary to walk along with your pack of sins on your back; you can now take a train, put your sins in the baggage car, and pick them up at the other end! Now there is a bridge built across the marshy Slough of Despair, and a tunnel bored right through the hill of Difficulty. So across the bridge and through the tunnel the train roars, carrying a delighted Hawthorne. Then, as the author gazes out the window, he sees two pilgrims traveling in the old fashioned way, on foot with their packs of sins on their backs. As the train roars by, Hawthorne hoots and jeers; how foolish, he cries, not to take advantage of modern conveniences!

Suddenly angelic voices rise above the noise of the locomotive. But when he looks outside, Hawthorne notes with dismay that the angels' songs of welcome are not for him, nor for anybody on the train, but rather for the two weary foot-pilgrims, who somehow have gotten ahead of the train, and are now entering happily into the Celestial City. At this moment, the engineer of the Celestial Railroad looks back at Hawthorne. It is the dragon Apollyon, symbol of Satan! He grins diabolically, winks at our author, and belches fire and smoke. At this moment, the Celestial Train veers off and heads straight toward the flaming caverns of hell. Hawthorne awakes with a quaking heart, and his last words are, "Thank God it was a dream!"

The trouble with the passengers on Hawthorne's train was that they believed there was some quick and easy way to salvation. Similarly, many students think there is a quick and easy way to knowledge. They think they can leapfrog the basics without penalty. The chief "leapfrog" techniques are ignoring directions, over-relying on computers, and cheating by "borrowing." According to most of my women friends, the male population is the best example of the first technique. "Witness the husband who spends hours trying to program his VCR," they say. "Only after all else has failed will he condescend to read the directions." I must confess that I had been guilty of this failing on more than one occasion.

One summer when we were at Hanover College in Indiana, Ginny and I drove to Louisville for dinner. I crossed the Ohio River on the bridge into the city, turned left, and in a minute or so found myself back on the same bridge, going *out* of the city. This happened twice. On the third try over the Ohio, we had to stop for a red light. Ginny, her eyes snapping, said, "Let's ask for directions." Before I could protest, she rolled down her window, and yelled to the driver of a huge truck next to us. "Hey," she said, "how do we get to the Golden Turtle restaurant?" The driver, a big guy with tattooed arms, quickly gave Ginny the directions, peering at me with some disdain as the light turned green and he roared off. It was mortifying, especially for a former navigator.

No question, the driver had a piece of information I lacked—the location of the restaurant and how to get there. But *information is not knowledge.* Knowledge involves understanding the facts or data, synthesizing them to reveal interrelationships, and then identifying the sources and significance of the information. A computer is a mechanism for processing information. Whether that information becomes knowledge depends on the person at the computer table. It is his mind, not the computer, that has the potential to achieve knowledge.

Thus the computer, even when linked to the Internet, is not a short cut to knowledge. According to articles appearing in the August 1997 issues of the *Chronicle of Higher Education*, there is even a question as to whether it is a short cut to comprehensive and reliable information. The first article, "Troubling Myths about On-line Information," is by William Miller, President of the Association of American Research Libraries. The second, "How the Web Destroys the Quality of Student Research Papers," is by David Rothenberg, a professor at New Jersey Institute of Technology. Mr. Miller states that much so-called Web information "is simply junk—neither current, objective, or trustworthy." Professor Rothenberg weighs in on the same side. He asserts that what passes for information on the Web is "simply advertising for information," that is, possible sources, unauthenticated summaries of summaries, "quips, blips, snippets, and pictures." Such a jumble, he contends, provides "fragmented and superficial" student papers.

According to our authors, over-reliance on the computer, even for information, is a mistake. Most serious Web material, they say, is in the form of journals, not books. Even so, only 4000 of the world's 150,000 journals are at this point electronically available. Trying to get even this partial and erratic information from the Web, insists Miller, is like attempting to drink from a fire hose. Any query precipitates a "torrent of data" —as many as 10,000 "hits" per inquiry, of which only a fraction may be helpful. And Rothenberg adds that computer "search engines" are closer to slot machines than library catalogues. From the above we must conclude that any decent town library contains valuable works that will never make the Web, and that its card catalogue, even if never computerized, will be a far better index to information than anything the Web can supply in the foreseeable future.

The third most popular method of "leapfrogging" the basics is cheating, or plagiarizing. According to *The American Freshman*, an annual survey of first year students, plagiarism has significantly increased during the last decade. The University of Delaware revamped its academic code in 1985, after the institution found that 78 percent of its students acknowledged cheating in one fashion or another. Guilty students at Delaware now receive a grade of XF on their transcripts, and can get the X removed only if they take and pass a course which includes ethics and time management. Other colleges could well consider the Delaware approach. At a minimum, through freshman orientation programs, colleges should aggressively address this problem, since it threatens to undermine any kind of meaningful education. Students can't learn by "borrowing" the knowledge of others. Knowledge is earned, not stolen. Taking the cheating route robs young people of the opportunity to grow.

According to recent educational journals, the number of students who do not regret cheating increasingly dismays college officers. But the sense of guilt and embarrassment often arises later. I recently talked with a city agency director who, as a Boy Scout, had twice failed to earn his merit badge in cooking. On the third try, he used his mother's dough, passed on the strength of *her* biscuits, and made Eagle Scout. At the time my friend viewed the deception as a trivial matter. But he confessed that now, many years later, he has an uneasy feeling about the incident, especially when asked to speak to a class of aspiring Eagle scouts. I suggested that perhaps he could atone by turning in his merit badge sash, but he didn't think that was funny.

Cheating in college creates an attitude that can become embedded in later life. Note the scientific careers recently destroyed by plagiarism, and the investment bankers and corporate officers who have been jailed for white-collar crimes. There is no "quick fix" to knowledge or to anything else that matters. It is simply a fact that you can't play a violin without first mastering the techniques peculiar to that instrument. Bypassing the basics, even if no cheating is involved, can lead to tragedy or comedy, but always to sloppy performance. On the comic side is the famous incident at Auburn University, where a new women's residence hall was under construction. Because the workmen installed one-way vision windows *the wrong way*, the occupants could not see out, but the campus folk could see in. Before the error could be corrected, males were coming from fifty miles away to look in. The football coach even had trouble getting his players to come to practice.

The foreman had obviously not read the directions, or if he had, he failed to pass them along to his colleagues. All of us are annoyed by sloppy performance, especially when we are the victims. But most of us admire outstanding performance, even when we are not the beneficiaries. College should teach us to take delight in anything done with professional skill, whether it be a nightclub performer's dancing, an engineer's suspension bridge, a jeweler's diamond cutting, or even a senior class prank.

When I was president at the University of Bridgeport, I used to make it a practice, early on the morning of each commencement, to visit the site and enjoy the orderly setting for the coming event—the dignitaries' platform positioned under its bright awning, the flags of the various student nationalities flapping in the breeze, the 6,000 chairs neatly arranged in sections and aisles to accommodate the procession of students and their proud and happy families. One year, however, as I made my early morning inspection, something seemed amiss. Some early arriving parents had surrounded a security guard, and were gesturing emphatically. Other parents were already in their seats, but glancing over their shoulders in bewilderment. As well they might be, because now the stage was *behind* them and they were facing in the opposite direction. Somehow, overnight, 6,000 chairs had been reversed and realigned in the same meticulous rows, aisles, and sections, but facing away from the stage. How could this have happened, given the heavy security around the courtyard?

We soon learned the answer. It had been a carefully planned prank, pulled off with the skill of a commando operation. One group of seniors had faked a fire alarm in a nearby dorm. This ruse drew off campus security long enough for another group to enter the courtyard and carry out their mission, which had been developed and secretly rehearsed over the preceding weeks. Even the security guards had to chuckle at the precision of this performance. Frankly, it was the high point of that year's commencement! Hopefully the "commandos" gave the same meticulous attention to their final exams.

Anything worth doing is worth doing well, even a college prank. I would rather hire a plumber whose pipes held water, than a noble philosopher whose thoughts leaked. Any job, done right, becomes important; the most menial jobs are often the most critical. In Eugene O'Neill's play *The Hairy Ape,* a stoker in the bowels of an ocean liner says to a well-dressed passenger who has asked to see the engine-room, "I'm at the bottom of things, lady. I make the whole thing tick." Like the stoker on O'Neill's ship, most of us want to be proud of our work, no matter what and where it is. See the work of a medieval craftsman in the darkest recesses of a Gothic cathedral. Why did he work so thoroughly when he knew that few would ever see what he did? Because he regarded his work as a reflection of his own self-respect and pride in craft.

This European pride in work was brought across the ocean to America. That is obvious in those four-story houses towering like Homeric giants in once-fashionable sections of Troy and Louisville. They were built to endure; they are residential Gibraltars, and they will last as long as Gibraltar lasts. Likewise, those graceful mansions in the restored sections of Savannah and Charleston prove that many American workmen have taken pride over the years in what they did. But somewhere along the line too many of our modern craftsman, symbolized by our Auburn University foreman, have forgotten the admonition of St. Paul to Timothy, "Be thou a workman that needeth not to be ashamed."

In the last analysis, shame comes from sloppiness, and pride from competence. Competence, in turn, comes from mastering the basics. Those who wish to follow Paul's admonition would do well to build a foundation in the fundamentals. Students who take the basics seriously, because their colleges do, reap disproportionate rewards by their upper-class years.

4

Saying What We Mean

*"Sir, the star of last year's Ziegfield Follies has just fallen
on the promenade deck and sprained her hip."*

ACH FIELD, LIKE nursing, engineering, or business, has a set of "basics" peculiar to itself. Nursing is
grounded in physiology, engineering in the hard sciences, and business in accounting, statistics, or management, depending on whom you
talk to. But the one basic principle common to all fields is communication. Without mastery of that skill we are dead in the water no matter what
line of endeavor we choose.

Communication of course includes listening and reading. Any worthwhile communications course will seek to empower students to read and
listen critically rather than passively, so that they can evaluate the degree
of fact and bias reflected in the interpretation of the issue at hand. But
this chapter focuses on speaking and writing, because these are the
aspects of communication that have created so much controversy in
our own time.

Long experience has taught me that effective communication requires that we speak or write in the way that each situation demands.
This does not mean that standards are abolished or are no longer ap-
plicable. There are still criteria for proper communication, but they have
changed. "Proper" used to mean strict adherence to certain 18th Century
rules. Now "proper" means saying or writing what is appropriate to the

time, place, audience and circumstance involved. Speed limits are a good analogy here. When we notice that the speed limit on some streets is 20 miles an hour and on others 50, we don't accuse the Police Chief of having no standards. Communication standards, like speed limits, vary with the situations in which we find ourselves.

In the 1950's, Charlton Laird wrote a provocative book, *The Miracle of Language,* which explains this viewpoint in greater detail. In the book, he relates an experience that happened during World War II, when he was working as a foreman in a shipyard. When he politely said, "Please pick up those [steel] bars," the workmen just stared at him. But when he preceded his request with an expletive and demanded sternly, "Pick up *them* bars," he suddenly got action. His point was that "them bars" might not have been acceptable on Beekman Place, or in an interview for a corporate management position, but it was very acceptable in the shipyard. It was language the men could understand; it *communicated* and therefore got the job done.

Language is the stuff of communication. The kind of language we use, and the way we structure it, determines whether our communication is effective or not. The traditional approach to communication has become a sham, because it teaches an artificial "classroom" language that bears little relation to what the teacher uses in the hall after the bell rings. Some years ago a group of high school teachers insisted that they were devotees of the 18th Century rules. So with their advance knowledge and consent, I conducted "Operation Earcock" for two weeks. Some of my students from the University of Cincinnati (where I was then a professor) shadowed the teachers in their daily work, and recorded their every comment. The compiled results were as expected. Like most educated people, the teachers frequently deviated from strict grammatical rules. They might have taught "with whom" in the classroom, but it was "Who you going with?" in the cafeteria.

If we want to communicate effectively, we must learn how language actually functions in the real world; not how ancient grammarians thought it should function. Modern deviations from 18th Century rules and vocabulary simply reflect the fact that every living language changes through the centuries. If we were to bring King Alfred, Chaucer, and Hemingway together, they would probably not understand each other. Three centuries ago, Alexander Pope rhymed "tea" with "way"; "penicillin" was not in the vocabulary of the *Beowulf* poet; "silly" meant unfortunate to Chaucer; and even more modern words like "fountain pen" and "ice box" are disappearing as we enter the 21st Century.

If language is the stuff of communication, words are the stuff of language. Hence it is crucial to realize that over time words change in social acceptability. "Ain't" was considered fashionable many years ago. In Falstaff's time, "wench" was a complimentary term for a young woman. "Bead" originally referred to prayer, then to the rosary used in prayer, and finally to jewelry. Similarly, the distinction between "*dis*interested" (objective) and *un*interested (uncaring) has sadly faded; and while "gay" once meant happy, it now connotes a sexual orientation. Meanwhile, many foreign words, or derivations of them, have flooded into English. To name only a few: pumpkin (French), gung-ho (Chinese), jazz (West African), honcho (Japanese), sauna (Finnish), harem (Turkish), phooey (German), calaboose (Spanish), hunky-dory (Dutch), coyote (Mexican), moccasin (Native American), and schnook (Yiddish).

Word and language changes are rarely reversed. Against historical and social forces, the old rules are like peashooters against a tank. Language cannot be frozen—neither the French Academy nor Samuel Johnson could succeed in doing so. English, especially American English, is adventurous and like the people who speak it, pluralistic and multi-faceted. Those who seek to control a living language through rules are destined to failure—they are trying to stir the ocean with a coffee spoon. Language must accommodate changing times and conditions to continue to be a vehicle for effective communication. Hence change is a sign of health, not corruption.

In our Age of Technology, where writing is often reduced to e-mail, speech, including ordinary conversation, has become the chief form of communication. The battle cry here is "Say what you mean." There must be a common understanding between what the speaker says and the listener hears, or confusion and even hostility can result. Some years ago, a woman at a party asked me what kind of navigator I had been in the war. "Celestial," I replied. She looked annoyed and said, "You're not very modest, are you?"

Much of the confusion in communication is caused by such double meanings in the use of words. One summer Stephen Leacock, the great Canadian humorist, signed on board the *Queen Mary* as *Dr.* Stephen Leacock, signifying his Ph.D. in Political Science. Halfway across the Atlantic a purser rushed up and asked, "Are you Doctor Leacock?" "I am indeed," replied our professor. "Well sir, the star of last year's *Ziegfeld Follies* has just fallen on the promenade deck and sprained her hip. Could you please come down to her room?" As Leacock tells it, he "sprang down to the woman's room like a startled gazelle." But he was sorely disappointed when he arrived. There, kneeling beside the bed and minutely inspecting the woman's hip, were *two* Doctors of Divinity who had beaten him to it.

Effective communication requires that our listener not only understand what we mean, but react accordingly. To achieve these ends, our speech must be appropriate, especially to the audience we are addressing. If our language is not acceptable to that audience, they will be alienated, and our chances of communicating effectively will be diminished. A case in point is so-called "Black English." Such speech might be effective communication in the ghetto, where it is in some measure socially accepted and understood. But it is a disastrous vehicle of communication for anyone who aspires to live and work in educated society. There are two audiences involved here, and the first is very different from the second. The best advice communication instructors can give students is simple: when in Rome, talk as the Romans do—if you want to be understood and accepted.

Throughout human history, the greatest religious leaders have been geniuses at adapting their language to their audiences. Jesus spoke in short parables which simple people could understand, parables of the mustard seed, the eye of the needle, the prodigal son. Moses, called upon to explain creation to an illiterate audience, shrewdly avoided giving a theological speech. Instead he described God as a laborer working for six days and resting on the seventh. St. Paul, addressing a group of Greeks on Mars Hill, deliberately quoted a Greek philosopher, Plotinus, to explain the way God permeates our daily lives.

Good talkers always adjust to their audiences, even today. It is important for colleges to provide opportunities for students to witness and practice this adaptability. Tom Hoving, the former director of the Metropolitan Museum and inventor of the "Big Apple" tag for New York, once gave a commencement address at UB that brought the senior class to its feet in a thunderous ovation. Why? Because he brilliantly adjusted his language and illustrations to the world of college seniors, comparing them in a dramatic closing to a rocket about to be launched at Cape Kennedy: "So it's five, four, three, two, one, zero—TAKE OFF!" Wow.

The reason we adjust our speech to our audience, and where appropriate to our location, is to achieve acceptance of our views, or to inspire some desired behavior. Recent scholarship suggests that many of us do a poor job in this regard. As Anita Wenden and Christine Schaffaer note in *Language and Peace*, inept language, even if unintentional, can cause misunderstanding, resentment, and even violence among those we seek to pacify. In another recent book, *You Just Don't Understand*, Deborah Tannen explains how relationships between men and women are complicated and even retarded by differences in their conversational styles. Such research makes us realize that language, to a frightening degree, shapes human relationships. The exhortation, "Watch your language!" shouted by a parent at a sassy teenager, also applies in the most sobering degree to all of us.

One of the most colorful aspects of speech, especially ordinary conversation, is slang and dialect. Instructors who want to enthuse students will follow the lead of professors at Chicago, Minnesota, and Emory Universities in giving these deviations a legitimate place in the teaching of language. In theory, slang is considered sub-standard English. But slang words are great social climbers. Certain "clipped words" like taxi, phone, and plane were socially unacceptable when first used, but have now become a solid part of informal speech. By contrast, some slang, including the jet set and campus variety, emerges briefly and then falls out of fashion forever. Nobody I know says "23 Skidoo" anymore, or even knows what it means.

Typically, slang consists of picturesque phrases which evoke an image, but whose literal translations do not convey their true meaning. Foreigners are constantly baffled or amused by such expressions as "pushing up daisies," "kicking the bucket," "off the wall," "screw loose," "wet blanket," "loose cannon," "laughing academy," "case the joint" and "up a creek without a paddle." The comic strip, *Gasoline Alley*, recently featured two Russians who were trying to understand American slang. "How can you *push up* daisies?" a puzzled Cambodian lady once asked. Over time, such expressions can become permanent parts of American conversation, even slipping into the speeches of presidents.

Consider an editor of the *Dictionary of the English Language* who was once asked what he thought of President George Bush's use of the expression "cool it" in a major speech. "It's fine with me," said the editor. "Now is not the time for the President of the United States to worry about the King's English. After all, we are living in an informal age. Politicians don't go around in top hats any more. There's no reason why the English language shouldn't wear sports clothes, too. I'm not saying the President should speak like an illiterate, but cool it is folksy, and the Chief Executive should be allowed to sound human."

Anyone interested in language can have a lot of fun with slang, and also with dialect, another part of sub-standard English. Dialect consists partly of accents restricted to a particular region. I used to be able to tell where persons were from just by asking them to pronounce words like *cement, idea, route, vase,* and *hair.* As we move further south in the U.S., for example, the word *hair* gradually becomes polysyllabic. In Tennessee, there are two syllables, and by the time you get to Alabama and Mississippi, there may be as many as three. When I was an aviation cadet in Tennessee, I had a tall, redheaded girl friend named Cliffordean Taggart. Many years later I returned to Nashville to give a lecture, and she was in the audience—now a plump platinum blonde, and mother of four. She rushed up afterwards, threw her arms around me and exclaimed, "Leland, you have *hay-ah!*" "Of course I have *hay-ah,*" I replied, imitating her Southern accent. "What did you expect?" Whereupon she introduced me to her husband, who was bald.

Peculiar word meanings are also a part of dialect. There should be opportunities in college for students to hear dialect, either directly or through recordings. As a case in point, if you ask for a "milkshake" within fifty miles of Boston, you will get exactly that—shaken milk—perhaps with some flavoring. The first time I got a milkshake at Bailey's (maybe it was Brigham's) in Boston, I took one swallow and asked the waitress, "Where's the ice cream?" "There's no ice cream in a milkshake," she said. "That's ridiculous," I replied. "Where do you come from, Samoa?" We argued vociferously in front of the customers, who couldn't figure out what the problem was. Finally it hit her. "Wait a minute," she said. "You want a *frappe!*" "What's a frappe?" I asked, mystified. "It's a milkshake with ice cream," she said. "But a milkshake *always* has ice cream!" I remonstrated. Eventually I realized you can't fight language. If you want a Baltimore "milkshake" in Boston, you had better order a frappe.

Dialect, along with outmoded historical forms (e.g. "five mile" down the road) should be enjoyed and respected, but is nonetheless part of sub-standard English—unless you live in or travel through the region where the dialect is spoken! Standard English, on the other hand, consists of acceptable formal and informal expression. Informal or "colloquial" English consists of those words and expressions that are appropriate to everyday educated conversation and informal writing. Formal English is more carefully structured, uses more Latinized words, and tends to lean toward the old traditional rules. Remember the high school teachers who consented to "Operation Earcock?" Without realizing it, they were teaching Formal English in the classroom, but using Informal English among themselves.

What we are really talking about here is "levels of usage." As noted earlier, effective communication is speaking or writing in the way that is most appropriate for the situation in which we find ourselves. Our language should be more formal for a United Nations speech than for a casual conversation in a locker room. Imagine how embarrassed we'd be if we got mixed up and used locker room language for a formal address, or vice versa! If colleges do nothing else in teaching communications, they must sensitize students to the reality of these usage levels.

How we speak and write is one of the most important behaviors others observe in us. For better or worse, our use of language has become a status symbol. More than any other symbol, effective communication makes us competitive, and assures us a reasonable quality of life. Unbelievably, some Marxist professors claim that Standard English is "an instrument of domination," helping to "sustain a rigid or evil class structure." The very opposite is the case. Standard English does not oppress minorities. On the contrary, it is the escape hatch from the ghetto. Of all the basics, communication is the most important tool for colleges to teach their students, and for students to master during the freshman and sophomore years. Without communication skills, it is impossible to discuss ideas effectively. And ideas are the be-all and end-all of the intellectual side of college life and of much that will happen afterward.

5

Competition of Ideas

"You talk about revolution when you haven't read Marcuse?"

ONE OF THE MAJOR obligations of a college or university is to assure that students work in a stimulating atmosphere of ideas. In a general sense, most colleges fulfill this obligation, if only because they cannot very well do otherwise. A lively faculty and student body help assure the needed atmosphere, even if an administration doesn't actively encourage it.

Diversity of faculty and students is as crucial to a real college as diversity of ideas. No school can be a free forum for competing thought if everyone within it is Marxist or Capitalist. Diversity of personnel guarantees a competition of ideas, while homogeneity retards it. For this reason, if for no other, Affirmative Action must be applied in student admissions, to assure that not only minorities but also international students are adequately represented on campus. To the extent that Federal or State law bans Affirmative Action, alternate models are available such as the "Operation Opportunity" program described in Chapter 1. A resurrected "Double O", like the original, would not be geared to race, but to under-achieving students, many of whom would be minorities who suffer from inadequate schooling or home environment.

What can be done with imaginative alternatives to Affirmative Action is illustrated by Texas A&M and the University of Texas at Austin.

Forced to abandon AA by State law, these institutions now offer "adversity scholarships" to the most needy students in the top 10 percent of selected high school graduating classes, regardless of the school's size or academic standing. The result has been little or no decline in the number of minority students at these institutions.

On a college campus, ideas most often take the form of issues, whereby two or more ideas, views, or solutions fight for favor among the campus community. When it comes to debating issues, no organization out-performs a university. Almost any day, at almost any college, we can find a formal or informal debate under way, sometimes with the aid of outside speakers and resource people. There is no restriction on locale for such discussions. They occur at student club meetings, dorm sessions, convocations, special forums, and over the lunch table. They also occur in classrooms when the issue is appropriate to the subject matter (and sometimes when it isn't).

At the typical college, issues tend to fall into three broad categories. First are those dealing with campus activities. Has the campus newspaper exceeded good taste by speculating on the Dean's sex life? Who publishes the campus newspaper, the students or the administration? How do we balance campus security with the need to use the city as a student laboratory? Is a college compromised by participating in government-sponsored research on, for example, military lasers, or syphilis among minorities? Why is the president off-campus so much, and therefore not available to talk with students? Alternatively, why is he *on* campus so much, rather than off in Washington or wherever raising funds? Why is tuition so high, why aren't there more black professors, why is the food so bad, why isn't there a day care center for student parents?

During my tenures as president at two institutions, co-ed dorms were one of the hottest campus life issues, especially among parents and alumni. When, at Alfred, I announced a new policy which placed males and females on alternate floors of certain dorms, some older women from a Florida alumni group protested, saying such arrangements were immoral, and they lay in wait for my next visit to Florida. When I arrived for a speech there, they climbed all over me, until I finally said, tongue in cheek, "Hey, wait a minute. Ever since we put women with men in these co-ed dorms, the men have dressed, spoken, studied, and generally behaved better. Why? Because women are the moral control in society. Left alone, men will misbehave, but with women, they become gentlemen. Ladies, I am seeking to develop *gentlemen* at Alfred University!" The older women, the complainers, sat speechless, unable to disagree with my thesis. After the applause, mostly from male alumni, one matron raised her hand and timidly said, "Well, Doctor, now that you put it that way, maybe *all* the dorms should be co-ed!"

Far removed from residence hall policies are the academic issues. Some of these are of a scholarly nature, and emerge in the classroom as the various academic disciplines are taught. Why is the picture of the Native American so distorted in early American history? How do we explain and define "black holes" in outer space? Who were the predecessors of modern art? Can genetic engineering be used to control the mind? Was Protestant thought influenced by Greek philosophy? Are jazz musicians the true inheritors of the early classical musicians? How successfully can free market concepts be merged with socialist economies? Have John Dewey's views been helpful or hurtful to American education? Professors should engage students in debating such questions, and the best ones do. The advance understanding should always be that the only "wrong" answer is the one unsupported by rational argument. The aim of college is to teach the students how to think, not what to think, because much of the information on which they base their views will have shifted or become obsolete by the time they take on their first jobs after graduation.

Then there are the practical curricular issues: How feasible is a "co-op/work study" approach for fields other than business and engineering? Would fine arts students benefit from a practical minor like industrial design? Should business programs be slanted toward venture management? Should we begin a new program in computer-aided design and manufacturing, or incorporate gerontology into the nursing program, or start black and/or women's studies, or adjust Western Literature to accommodate Eastern classics? What about a liberal arts core? What should be its requirements and cohesive principle? Who determines what is "politically correct" and its proper relationship, if any, to the college curriculum? Is "men's studies," recently introduced by Hobart and William Smith Colleges in New York, a backlash against or a natural extension of political correctness? All of these issues are likely to arouse heated debate, especially among faculty.

When I was a young professor at Hanover College in Indiana, a hotly debated controversy broke out over whether an English competence test would be required for graduation. The argument climaxed at a winter faculty meeting. The public has no idea what goes on at such an assembly. If they did, they would forget about movies, the World Series, and television as major forms of entertainment. The particular subject on the agenda on this occasion was the adoption of an all-college policy on fundamental English, the artistic handiwork of a frail little committee consisting of a zoology professor, a sociology professor, and me.

Seldom, I think, in the college world's history, have so few been abused by so many. It was obvious from the Dean's opening prayer, in which he asked that a spirit of quiet tolerance prevail, that the faculty were in one of their "you-read-it-and-then we'll-tear-it-apart" moods. The professorial avant-garde ripped into Item No. 1 of the proposed policy: whether students who made a "D" in English Composition should take remedial English. First, they wanted to know, what is a "D" anyway? This line of questioning broke down into three separate squabbles, all going on somewhat bewilderingly at the same time, and dealing, as far as I could ascertain, with grading systems, the honor code, and a defense of elementary teachers of grammar, especially a certain Miss Whoop, whom one of the Education professors knew personally and defended heatedly.

Eventually the "raging Logomachy"—as a classics professor later described it in the official minutes—descended upon Item No. 2: that "faculty members shall penalize students for faulty English." Here the argument snagged on a grammatical point. Should the statement use "shall" or "will"? When a voice of wisdom, as I recall, mine, broke through the confusion and offered the argument that "shall" implied do-or-die determination rather than mere future probability, Item No. 2 fell like a termite ridden oak, branded as a fascist statement aimed at dominating the minds of free-thinking men.

These explosions were mere monastic meditations compared to the thunderous discussion that followed on Item No. 3: "An English Competency Test should be required for graduation." The vocal opposition posed a profound question—"Why should there be a required competence test in English any more than in psychology or chemistry?" Friends of the test asserted that English is the common instrument of every field and therefore the most vital subject of all. Others, taking this as a personal affront, rose and defended their subject fields with inspired eloquence. In fact, as one botany instructor observed later, they were so eloquent, that about midway through their speeches, they realized they were making a magnificent case for the supreme value of vocabulary, diction, and proper usage.

At this point, a music professor suggested that faculty meetings be open to students with a fifty-cent admission charge. This suggestion reduced the assemblage to hysterical laughter, leaving everyone limp and exhausted, like a collective worn-out boxer at the end of the fifteenth round. In the end the entire matter was dumped back to the committee for re-consideration and the meeting adjourned.

Beyond curricular controversies like English competence tests, there are the social or public affairs issues. National issues debated on campus today might include abortion rights, single parenting, pre-marital sex, the status of women and minorities, political campaign reform, drug abuse, gun control, animal rights, poverty, and the youth/age conflict. Regarding this latter issue, one question is whether a shrinking corps of young people can or should be required to shoulder the Social Security and Medicare tax burden for an expanding cohort of senior citizens. In the international arena, students and faculty seem especially concerned with environmental collapse, human rights, foreign trade, repression of dissidents in China, the Israeli-Arab conflict, post-apartheid South Africa, and over-population.

Politicians, of whatever label, are especially controversial on campuses. I remember an opening convocation at Alfred at which the conservative Senator John Tower spoke. It was the late 1960's, during the "student unrest" period, when a lot of students were protesting America's involvement in Vietnam. When Tower joined his audience after the speech to greet students and shake hands with parents, a small group of so-called radicals surrounded him. The leader, a white student with a pseudo-Afro haircut, had two small American flags stuck in his hairdo. "Mr. Tower is a Republican," I said to this student, "Are you a Democrat?" "No," he growled. "I'm a revolutionary." "Really!" I replied. "Then you must know Herbert Marcuse's book, *Repressive Tolerance.*" "No, I haven't read it," he confessed. "What?" I thundered, pretending anger. "You talk about revolution when you haven't read Marcuse? How can we have a meaningful dialogue?" The kid grinned sheepishly, and drifted away with his friends.

The most volatile issues at any college are those which cut across constituencies—like ROTC at the University of Bridgeport, for instance.

There had never been a ROTC unit at UB. The Army was now offering one. The matter began as a curricular proposal under review by the administration, but it became a campus life concern when the student newspaper wrote an editorial denouncing "bayonets on campus." Since by now the issue had attracted national attention, I referred it to the University Senate, which was composed of administrators, faculty and students.

The question was simple. Should we accept the Army's offer? The Senate debated it for four months. Finally I received a phone call from the general in charge of ROTC. "What's going on at your place?" he asked. "Do you want this unit or not? If you don't, we're giving it to Southern Connecticut State." This barb dug deep, because SCS was one of our main public competitors. "I have a problem, General," I replied. "The Senate's still debating the issue." The General got quite emotional. "The Senate!" he screamed. "How in hell did *they* get involved?

"Not the U.S. Senate, General, the UB Senate," I replied. This clarification did not seem to calm him. "The UB Senate, eh," he said sarcastically. "Look Doctor, who is running the show up there, you or your Senate?" "Well, that's a good question," I replied. "My trustees ask me that all the time." By now the General was really up tight. "Okay, Mr. President," he said, "Either accept the ROTC program now, or it goes to SCS." I started to protest, but he hung up. With that I went to the Senate. "Sorry, we're still debating," they said. "No, you've just finished," I replied. UB accepted ROTC. Even in a free forum of conflicting ideas, there come times when decisions must be made.

Of course there was an uproar. The Senate issued a manifesto denouncing my totalitarian tactics. But eventually it all blew over. If a president can just hold on for a while, another issue will pop up to overshadow the prior one. At colleges, issues are in a constant state of flux. Some, like South Africa, remain but change focus. Others, like co-ed dorms, disappear and then re-surface in a different form. Not long ago at the University of South Carolina, and more recently in the Northeast, co-cd dorms have again become a controversial issue, on the grounds that they allegedly encourage poor study habits. As a result, some institutions have established "quiet dorms," where the opposite sex is forbidden to enter.

Still other issues remain forever. Among the latter is the English Competence Test. It pops up all the time, most recently at the City University of New York. For many years, CUNY had used such a test to determine whether new students were proficient enough to take college level courses. However, in spring 1997 the institution announced that the test would become a condition for graduation, beginning with Hostas Community College in the South Bronx. Unfortunately, only 13 of 104 mostly Hispanic students passed the test, provoking a parental storm of protest which rocked both the administration and local politicians. As Yogi Berra used to say, "It's deja vu all over again."

Another perennial controversy is "bad food." The alleged inadequacy of institutional food has been the eternal student complaint since Plato formed his academy. Soon after I returned to UB as president, having been a dean earlier, I made it a point to visit the student cafeteria at dinnertime. By student standards the meal was exceptional: steak, French fries, salad, apple pie á la mode. "What's the problem?" I queried. "Why all the griping?" They looked at me with resignation. "They knew you were coming," one of them said. I was embarrassed by this response, because it was true. "Okay," I said, "Next time I'll drop in without warning." And I did. And what did I find on the student's supper trays? Steak, French-fries, salad, apple pie á la mode. "Now what's the problem?" I asked. "No one knew I was coming this time." The students were shaken. Finally a young woman said, "You just lucked out. You should have been here yesterday, or the day before." She was probably right. But no student ever complained to me about food again.

Given the bewildering maze of college issues, it is not an exaggeration to suggest that a typical college is a microcosm of the same debates taking place in the larger world. An excited sophomore once exclaimed to me, "College is an intellectual candy store." If so, it is merely a reflection of that larger "candy store" beyond the campus. The problem with both "stores" is the same: too many sweets. Those who gorge get indigestion. Counselors and faculty should aid newcomers in sorting out the issues, and help them develop informed stands on a few which seem most relevant for the student involved. Otherwise the student will become emotionally and intellectually overwhelmed. I once asked William Carlos Williams why another noted poet, Ezra Pound, went insane. "He cared too much," Williams replied. "He got personally involved in everything."

A college must be willing to address a variety of issues, and encourage similarly varied responses. Assuming a spectrum of opinions, there must be among all campus members a spirit of affectionate disagreement, of cheerful acknowledgment that differing perspectives spring from the differing approaches of the academic disciplines. Newman exalts such an atmosphere in his *Idea of a University*. Faculty and students alike are described there as seeking, "for the sake of intellectual peace, to adjust the claims of their various subjects." "In the process," says Newman, "they learn to respect, to consult, to aid each other." Would that this were always so!

To the extent that is humanly possible, college should be a place where ideas are shared, exchanged, and debated without rancor or personal abuse. Threats, demands, ultimatums, and disruptions are unacceptable at an educational institution. A college, if true to itself, will protect the right of every idea to have its day. This principle of tolerance is central to the college's mission. Our Congress and other institutions might reject unpopular ideas, or views that are repugnant to the majority. But these are the very ideas that a college should cherish, for the simple reason *they may be right.*

In the 16th Century, the prevailing view held that the sun rotated around the earth. When Copernicus arrived at the contrary view, he feared persecution from the church and other authorities. He therefore confined his thoughts to brief notes, shared them with only a few trusted friends, and deliberately obscured his authorship of the new concept. Similarly, in the 19th Century, surgical patients died at an appalling rate from hospital gangrene and similar infections. Joseph Lister concluded that bacteria, which could be controlled by antiseptics as simple as soap, caused these fatal infections. This view was ridiculed for more than a decade, and rejected by the Royal College of Surgeons. But today Lister is a hero. His ideas form the very basis of antiseptic medical practices.

In our own century, Eugene Debs was jailed as a radical, and Norman Thomas dismissed as an egghead, both for their advocacy of socialist principles. But many of their ideas have been stolen and enacted into law by both major political parties. Thus, when astronomers like Harlow Shapely envision "rooted dogs and walking trees" on other planets, we can smile, but it may be wise not to snicker. What is far out today may be gospel tomorrow. Nowhere should the commitment to address unconventional ideas, especially those opposed by powerful forces, be stronger than at an institution of higher learning.

Unfortunately, some colleges seek to limit ideas to those compatible with some part of the political or religious spectrum. Some years ago, when I was teaching at Hanover, a Presbyterian school, there were calls for the expulsion of a Moslem woman who questioned the resurrection of Jesus. More recently, Catholic University released a distinguished professor, because his views departed from the Vatican's. In a similar vein, the Georgia Baptist Convention in 1997 accused R. Kirby Godsey of "heresy" for his views in the book *When We Talk About God, Let's be Honest.* The strange thing here is that the author is the president of Mercer University, a Baptist institution! Such attempts to limit thought violate the desired nature of higher education.

More often than not, beliefs forged in the furnace of challenge will be strengthened, not weakened. Contrariwise, ideas kept in a vacuum, untested by opposition, collapse quickly when a real threat emerges. A college administrator can perform no greater disservice than attempting to protect students from rival views. Such efforts weaken their capacity to cope with the intellectual and spiritual doubts they will inevitably face in later life. No literary work makes this point more forcefully than Mark Twain's *The Man that Corrupted Hadleyburg.* The town of the title is a virtuous but isolated community, where people have never been permitted to confront evil. As a result, they fall easy prey to an insidious stranger who sets out to corrupt the community.

During the "student unrest" period of the 1960's, when I was president of Alfred University, some students and faculty sought to eliminate rival views by imposing their own ideas on everyone else. They sought to force the university community to vote against the government's policy in Vietnam. Perhaps without realizing it, they were trying to politicize the institution—to make it a propaganda vehicle for their own point of view.

Alarmed by these developments, I called the faculty into special session to advise them of the situation. In substance, this is what I said:

> As I understand the university, it is a protective shield beneath which all points of view can be expressed and cherished. Unlike a political party or a church, its mission is not to support a campaign platform or to preach some particular gospel. Its mission is rather to tolerate every conceivable shade of opinion, and to subject each such opinion to rational analysis, regardless of whether

such opinions find favor with trustees, corporations, or other funding sources.

A majority faculty vote against the Vietnam War has one obvious expectation, and that is to intimidate the minority into silence—through fear, shame, or embarrassment. To take such a vote is to generate among that minority the uneasy feeling that the university does after all have an "official line". . . .

I will fight any attempt to politicize this institution, on this issue or any other. To put the matter in a more positive vein, I will exert every effort to maintain the dynamic neutrality of Alfred University. My aim is to keep this institution neutral, for the simple reason that corporate neutrality is the prerequisite to academic freedom. Only through such a stance are students and faculty guaranteed the unhampered right to advocate their own ideas.

When I finished the speech and sat down, I was amazed at the reaction. The faculty abruptly stood as one body, and for a moment I feared they were coming after me. But no, they were giving me a standing ovation. They subsequently endorsed the speech by a vote of 118 to 3. Now that kind of vote is okay! My words were carried by national media and reprinted in the *Congressional Record*. The speech is as pertinent today as it was then.

6

Getting Curious

"Okay, wise guy, I give up. What did you do with the ship?"

THERE IS NOTHING like a competition of ideas to awaken or expand students' curiosity. From curiosity all else follows. A searching mind is of course an asset in any chosen profession, but it is equally critical in preparing for the world beyond work. In either sphere, curiosity is a priceless commodity.

Recently NBC gambled $40 million on a four-hour movie adaptation of *The Odyssey,* Homer's epic adventure story, and the ancient forerunner of Stephen Spielberg's *Jurassic Park.* When it comes to curiosity, colleges could find no better role model for their students than Homer's hero Ulysses, who spends ten years fighting the Trojan War and ten more returning to Ithaca and his queen, Penelope. During a turbulent homeward journey, he undergoes every adventure the fertile mind of Homer could invent. He fights the god Poseidon, outwits the one-eyed giant Cyclops, survives a shipwreck which drowns others, escapes from the evil sorceress Circe, and eventually comes to the island of Calypso, the ancient Greek equivalent of Madonna. With far greater willpower than we non-legendary people have, Ulysses spurns her offer of eternal youth and continues on toward his island home.

It is at this point that Ulysses comes to the island of the Lotus-eaters. These strange folk eat almost nothing but lotus leaves, which so alters their mental state that they only wish to live languid, lazy lives, drowsing under perfumed trees. Their message is the same as that of the pessimist A.E. Housman, who wrote: "Lie down, lie down, young yeoman, what use to rise and rise? Rise man a thousand mornings, yet down at last he lies." Ulysses, intrigued by the lotus-eaters, observes them carefully and spots their central flaw. They have no intellectual curiosity. They read nothing, discuss nothing, have no interest in the world around them. They are empty people—intellectual and moral zeroes. Whenever our hero tries to interest them in matters of importance all they say is, "Go away, leave us alone!" Unfortunately, two of Ulysses men eat the lotus, and immediately succumb to the same loss of curiosity. Fearful that his whole crew will be similarly seduced, Ulysses orders them to the ship and flees away with the first good breeze.

The moral in this episode, written 3000 years ago, is still relevant today, as the popularity of NBC's adaptation suggests. There are still Lotus-eaters around—both on and off campus. Just like their ancient counterparts, they are passive beyond description. We can detect the student Lotus-eater by his classroom behavior. After the third or fourth week, he begins slowly to open his mouth and slide back on his spine with a sort of fishy, glass-like stare. This physical posture reflects his educational philosophy. He believes that the professor is a big mother bird, and that he is a tiny baby bird. As he sees it, the teaching and learning process consists of the mother bird depositing the worm of wisdom in the baby bird's mouth. And the baby bird's got to lean back and open his mouth to receive the worm of wisdom, doesn't he?

A more recent Lotus-eater type doesn't even bother to come to class. Having capitulated to the Internet, he has lost all powers of sociability. Hypnotized by his PC, that electronic "Cyclops" with the giant square eye, he surfs for hours at a time, sliding from site to site at the click of his magic mouse. Hooked on the Web in his dark dorm cave, he ignores parents, roommates, friends, clubs, classes and the college at large. In short, he has become an Internet addict, a computer bum, an almost certain dropout. This type of Lotus-eater must be sharply distinguished from the admirable student who uses the computer as a tool for research, while continuing to be a constructive and out-going member of the college community.

In fairness to students, there are also faculty members who have eaten the lotus. Few of them even have a computer, much less being hypnotized by it. They are described by Brenda Miller Power of the University of Maine in a recent issue of the *Chronicle of Higher Education*. According to Power, these professorial Lotus-eaters "teach with syllabi that they haven't revised in years. They rarely read a journal or attend a faculty meeting. They stopped spending much time in their offices decades ago. . . . They blithely ignore their responsibilities to the institution, students, taxpayers, and other faculty members. Should someone be allowed to collect $70,000 a year, plus benefits, for that level of labor?"

In his poem "Ulysses," Alfred Tennyson picks up the story where Homer left off. He imagines that Ulysses, having returned to Ithaca, kills Penelope's suitors, resumes his kingship, rules for twenty years, and becomes increasingly bored. Finally, at the age of eighty, he decides to summon his old friends from the Trojan War to join in one last adventure. As the old men who were once his young companions stand beside him, Ulysses challenges them to seek beyond the horizon, Tennyson's apt metaphor for knowledge, because both keep slipping away as we approach them, so we never get there. The more we learn, the more there is to learn. In that spirit Ulysses says, at the end of the poem, "Come, my friends, 'tis not too late to seek a newer world." The old warriors jump into the boat, grab the oars, and stroke off into the setting sun.

Even in these modern times of living longer and doing more in advanced years, it might strain credulity to believe that one could embark on *Odyssey*-like adventures of the mind at the age of eighty. For doubters, the case of Israel Zimmerman is instructive. His story was told in the *New York Times,* April 10, 1972, under the headline, "3,991 Get Degrees in Heavy Downpour."

> Israel Zimmerman, an 81-year old retired laborer who was graduated from high school at the age of 70, was one of yesterday's recipients of a bachelor's degree in modern languages from Brooklyn College. He achieved a 3.0 grade index out of a possible 4.0. He now plans to pursue graduate studies.

As we read Homer, Tennyson, and the Brooklyn College article, we get the distinct impression that, for Ulysses and Zimmerman, intellectual curiosity was the desire to gain new knowledge, not in order to do anything with it, but just for the joyful experience of learning something new. Both seem to be saying that curiosity is for enriching minds, not enhancing work. There is some merit in this position. In the long run, a rich mind might be more profitable, at least in terms of personal satisfaction. As Cardinal Newman said in his *Idea of a University*, "Knowledge is capable of being its own end. Any kind of knowledge is its own reward."

My father and I differed frequently on the merit of Newman's viewpoint. When I was a young professor, I spent three summers exploring the Brontës, the 19th Century Yorkshire novelists. It was a joyful experience. After much research, I concluded that Charlotte Brontë had written *Wuthering Heights,* not her sister Emily, as commonly believed. The last summer I was working on this project, my father caught up with me. "What's all this about the Brontës?" he asked. I said, "Dad, I've discovered that Emily did *not* write *Wuthering Heights."* To which he replied, 'So what? Who cares? What are you going to do with it?" Another summer in graduate school, I learned Old English, a Germanic dialect. I had no intention of using this knowledge, but it was a lot of fun. So I came home and said to my father, "Dad, how would you like to hear a little Old English?" "What's Old English?" he asked. I replied by quoting the first line of *Beowulf,* 'Hwat, We Gâr-dena in Gear-dâgum." At this he leapt to the kitchen, poured himself a glass of bourbon, came back, took a huge gulp, and then gasped weakly, "But what are you doing to *do* with it?"

Embarrassed by the irrelevancy of my learning, at least from my father's perspective, I determined to find some practical way to apply my esoteric knowledge of the Brontës or Germanic Old English. The opportunity finally came. After Dad passed away, and after I became a college president at Alfred, my first official function was to attend an investment committee meeting in New York. Equitable Life Assurance's austere boardroom, where the meeting was held, would have been familiar to my father. Finally I was dealing in his milieu of stocks and bonds. The committee chairman said, "Leland, as this is your first function, would you care to say something?" I said, "Yes sir. What I would care to say is, 'Hwat, We Gâr-dena in Gear-dâgum.' " The trustees looked startled and said, "What does that mean?" "Loosely translated," I said, "it means 'If my father could only see me now!'" So I *did* do something with my Old English! I used it as the introductory comment at an investment committee meeting.

But let's not get carried away here. Newman said that knowledge is *capable* of being its own end. He said we didn't need to *do* something with it to make it worthwhile. But he did *not* say that it had no other purpose. Without doing something with certain kinds of knowledge, we could not resolve our personal problems and our careers would be a shambles. Thus, curiosity, the precursor of knowledge, is pre-requisite to a fruitful life, not just because it brings us inner joy, but also because it enhances our work and therefore our contribution to society.

In the last analysis, curiosity is nothing more than the desire to learn, even at the risk of humiliation and embarrassment. It is the spirit of the parrot on the ocean liner. This parrot's cage was in the ship's lounge where a third-rate magician performed each afternoon. Being much cleverer than the magician, the feathered intellectual had figured out all the tricks. When the magician suddenly produced a red handkerchief in his hand, the parrot screeched, "Cloth up sleeve; cloth up sleeve!" When the conjurer pulled a rabbit out of a hat, the parrot would give him away by bellowing, "Fake lid, fake lid!" If the magician ostentatiously drew the ace of spades from a carefully shuffled deck of cards, the parrot would scream, "All cards same, all cards same!" Understandably, a mutual hatred grew between the magician and the parrot. Then one afternoon in the middle of the voyage the ship developed a bad leak, broke apart, and sank. The parrot and the magician coincidentally wound up hanging onto opposite ends of the same bit of flotsam. For five days, they floated in silence, glaring at each other, but saying nothing. Finally the parrot couldn't stand it any longer. He stopped glaring at the magician, swallowed his pride, and weakly said, "Okay, wise guy, I give up. What did you do with the ship?"

That was a hard question for the parrot to ask! He had figured out every other trick the magician had performed. But this one had him stumped. Intellectual curiosity is the attitude of the parrot, willing to endure humiliation, willing to risk exposing ignorance, in an effort to learn. In my first year as a professor, a student phoned a colleague of mine late one night wanting to probe further into a problem they had discussed in class that morning. My friend tried to put him off, urging that they take up the discussion in his office the next day. But the student said, "Sir, I don't mean to inconvenience you, but I would sleep better if I could get some answers now." My colleague thought a moment and replied, "I understand; come on over and we'll talk about it." They did, far into the night. Later the student said he had gained a mind-enriching experience that would stay with him for the rest of his life. If he had waited until morning, he said, when his curiosity wasn't piqued, he might have missed it.

This kind of curiosity Albert Einstein called "holy." The scientist said that we are most divine when we are most curious. I don't know whether that theology is sound, but I'm convinced that all of us, insofar as we possess minds and personalities, have at hand an empty barrel when we are born. As we grow older, everything we come into contact with—everything we see, touch, learn, or read—all goes into the barrel. If we reach out with curiosity and seek for things profound, these things go into the barrel. But if we let the trite, superficial world hem us in on all sides, if we succumb to that world, then the contents of our barrel won't be worth much at the end. Suppose that at Judgment Day we were asked to turn our barrels upside down. Would we be embarrassed or proud at what spilled out? Would there be television beer ads in there, or paintings by Raphael and Rembrandt, or what?

Students who resolve to be aggressively curious, in the spirit of the parrot, will find that curiosity nudged and provoked by the competition of ideas, described in Chapter 5 as the essence of any lively institution. Their curiosity will be further broadened and deepened by exposure to a liberal arts program, where introductory courses are required in all the major areas of learning. These general education requirements can often be found in small colleges that may not be known well nationally, such as Centre in Kentucky, Kalamazoo in Michigan, Huron in South Dakota, Millsaps in Mississippi, Rockford in Illinois, Eckerd in Florida, and William and Mary in Virginia. Glenn Close, an alumna of the latter institution, was a recent commencement speaker at her alma mater and commented, "I've always been thankful that I didn't go to a fancy acting school, but that I came here and received a liberal arts education. The people who taught us—many of whom remain treasured friends—gave me what a good grounding in liberal arts should give everyone: an undying curiosity about the subjects taught."

Institutions like William and Mary also feature residential living, which provides a further stimulus for a budding curiosity. Melissa McGarry was the first undergraduate to win the coveted $50,000 Ettinger Scholarship from the Educational Foundation of America. In 1993, as a Colgate senior, she wrote me a letter, which stated in part: "Dormitory life is a learning experience. I have spent hours with a chemistry major who lives upstairs as he explained his senior research, while he has listened to me explain connections between the works of certain poets and composers. On a more leisurely note, my roommate taught me how to knit, and in return she can now hum the major themes of Mahler's First Symphony!"

Melissa points up the value of an atmosphere created by broad educational requirements. In such an environment, the history major will at first feel ignorant when his physics-centered roommate discourses on the dissipation of mass into energy; the biology student will be equally baffled initially by a philosophy major's exposition on Plato's Realm of Ideas. But the basic curiosity of these students, incubated through this kind of environment and nurtured by an enthusiastic faculty, will produce graduates who will continually probe and test and ask questions as they seek more knowledge on their own.

Intellectual curiosity, once awakened, becomes the catapult for a lifetime of learning. Those who get curious possess a motive power that protects them from the listlessness of the Lotus-eaters and impels them ceaselessly toward new adventures of the mind. As Ulysses and Israel Zimmerman knew, there is no age limit for embarking on such adventures. It is never too late to start toward the horizon. But those young people who become curious in college have a special advantage. Their momentum begins early, and the new worlds they can conquer are almost endless.

7

Cultivating Our Emotions

"All the way Choo-Choo, all the way Choo-Choo."

IN HAWTHORNE'S *Ethan Brand*, the title character broods so much on evil that he sees Satan in the fire of his own limekiln. Hypnotized by the vision, he leaps into the flames and is burned to ashes. The next morning the neighbors find only his heart, so stone hard it would not burn. This parable points up the danger of developing only our intellectual side. Intellectual curiosity is indispensable for a meaningful life. But it must be matched by the cultivation of our "affective side," of our feelings and emotions. Only by keeping the two in balance can we avoid the kind of warped psyche that destroyed Brand.

By cultivation of our emotions, I mean finding a middle way between "letting it all hang out" on the one hand, and unnatural suppression on the other. The former is unwise, the latter unhealthy. In ancient Rome, the slave Epictetus, a Stoic philosopher, was dragged before the emperor, flanked by two guards who were twisting his arms. "If they keep doing that," Epictetus told the emperor, "they'll break my arms." Whereupon two sharp cracks reverberated through the hall. "You see," said the Stoic, "I told you." Few of us could or should emulate Epictetus' stoicism, and at the other extreme, none of us should let emotions overwhelm our reason. What we should do is value emotions as an important part of our personalities, and seek to channel them toward constructive ends.

For the greater part of their existence, colleges and universities have largely ignored the emotional side of students, regarding it as irrelevant to higher education. When the poet John Milton attended Cambridge University in the 17th Century, there were no deans of student affairs, no counseling staff, no career placement centers. When the relevance of emotion for education was finally recognized in this century, counseling in all its various forms became a major component of college administration. Today, there is a tacit division of labor on college campuses: counselors see to the emotional well being of students, and the faculty handle development of their intellect.

However, this division of responsibility is likely to change in the next decade. Recent behavioral research reveals that the original brain, at the upper stem of the spine, was essentially "emotional" in nature. In the present state of evolution, this "emotional brain" impacts significantly on the larger, later evolving "intellectual" brain. This basic emotional function, if properly nurtured, includes persistence, self-discipline, compassion, and social deftness—the qualities that characterize those who excel in the workplace and in human relationships. Lack of this "emotional intelligence," as psychologist Daniel Goleman calls it in his recent book, sabotages the intellect and ruins careers. While Goleman is saying that the intellect has an emotional base, Helen Fisher of Rutgers takes the opposite view, that emotion (especially lust and love) are grounded in the brain's chemistry. But both are really saying the same thing, that intellect and emotions are closely allied.

Given the results of such research, the time has come for faculty to get involved with their students' emotional development. Few colleges have ever designed a conscious and explicit *educational* program to develop the affective side of their students' personalities, yet many of the resources for such an effort are available on almost any campus. One way to develop the affective side of one's nature, for example, is to study the visual or performing arts, to attend campus events such as concerts, exhibitions, poetry readings, and the like, or to paint or perform or play a musical instrument oneself. Two of the most balanced persons I ever knew were William Carlos Williams, a pediatrician who wrote marvelous poetry, and Karl Larsen, a physicist who played the violin.

The only musical instrument I ever attempted was the bugle. It has only nine notes, so any mistake is jolting, especially if you are playing "Taps." My mother so hated this instrument that she made me practice in a closet, preferring my asphyxiation to her listening. At best I became a mediocre bugler, but the experience gave me at least a minimal appreciation of the skill required to play the trumpet parts in Sousa's "Stars and Stripes Forever." More important, I was privileged to learn the two most beautiful bugle calls, "Tattoo" and "Lights Out," played at intervals after dusk and before "Taps." Though sixty years ago, I can still remember going to bed at Camp Linstead in Maryland. Lying on my bunk, I would listen to those wistful yet consoling calls wafting softly through the woods, played by a Scout bugler from fifty yards away. The notes, soulful and haunting, never failed to bring a chill to my spine. Even at fourteen years of age, I was enthralled by them. They seemed to say, "Rest now. Peace is here. Tomorrow will be another glorious day." Maybe this was my first unconscious effort to cultivate my own emotions.

If I had the power, I would require all students to take at least one course in art, theater, or music, even at colleges that lack a liberal arts core. The arts are a kind of emotional chiropractor: they manipulate, massage, and exercise our emotions, and in so doing not only calm our tensions, but help us to understand the feelings of others. We are awed when we view Botticelli's *Birth of Venus* (popularly called "Venus on a half shell"); moved to tears by a performance of Arthur Miller's *Death of a Salesman;* excited by the clarion call of Louis Armstrong's trumpet; enraptured by the strains of a Beethoven symphony.

Music has a particularly powerful impact on our emotions, because it transcends language. The recent film, *Paradise Road*, tells the true story of a group of women captured by the Japanese after the fall of Singapore in 1942. To raise morale, the women formed a "voice orchestra" and hummed the notes of Ravel's "Bolero" and Dvorak's "New World Symphony." The behavior of the Japanese soldiers toward their prisoners softened as they recognized the similarity between what the women were humming and their own Japanese folk songs. Sidney Lanier was right on target when he ended his poem "Symphony" with the line, "Music is Love in search of a word."

Balancing intellect and emotion can also be achieved through participation in sports. Colleges should require that students gain by graduation some degree of proficiency in at least one "lifetime sport," such as tennis, golf, swimming, sailing, or jogging. After all, the liberal arts originated with the Greeks, who were high on nurturing both mind *and* body. Colleges should also urge students to play or support at least one team sport. It need not be varsity athletics. It can be an intra-mural team or a pick-up game in the dorm courtyard. Any team sport, played or watched anywhere, can arouse the whole gamut of emotions from exultation to despair, for spectators as well as players.

When I was a graduate student at the University of North Carolina, I kept to my library carrel all day long, trying to write my dissertation. I was well on the way to becoming another Ethan Brand, all erudition and no feeling. One week, after much urging, I reluctantly agreed to accompany a friend to a football game. These were the days when Charlie "Choo Choo" Justice, UNC's All-American triple threat quarterback, was thrilling the sports world. He could do everything—pass, kick, block, run—especially run. Week after week he would stand back to receive a kick, then shift and dodge all the way to the rival team's goal, reversing field several times in the process and leaving would-be tacklers gasping and supine on the turf. Having watched Justice for two games, I suddenly found myself, to my own amazement, joining the frenzy of the other fans as they screamed, "All the way, Choo Choo, all the way Choo Choo!"

Choo Choo was obviously good for my emotions. But he was also good for my dissertation. After the emotional catharsis of watching him run, the writing of my dissertation began to go better! Therein lies an art that is not in the curriculum. Sometimes we plug away so long and hard that we reach diminishing returns. Redoubling our effort only makes things worse. We have run into a mental wall, and are getting nowhere. When that happens, the best thing is to *back off and relax.* Play tennis, ride a bicycle, take a nature walk, attend a jazz concert—or go see Choo Choo. Recreation is the key to the art of backing off. Once we've veered away and then swung back, we often find that the wall has disappeared.

Arts and sports are two ways of developing the "emotional" side of our personalities. Still another way available through campus life is establishing friendships. Genuine friendships require a significant degree of emotional commitment. In this area, as opposed to the casual acquaintanceships of the classroom, students usually receive only the vaguest kind of guidance. Dean's offices can offer little more than "damage control," because even today, when we are supposed to be psychologically hip, 80 percent or more of students are embarrassed to be seen consulting a counselor. Colleges which are really serious about "affective education" will offer an elective course in "Love and Friendship," or at least include similar material in the freshmen orientation program. In fact, some colleges now do so.

If I were to develop such a course, the first point I would discuss would be what forms the basis of friendship. When Miranda first sees the handsome Ferdinand in Shakespeare's *The Tempest*, she exclaims, "Nothing ill can dwell in such a temple." This idea is pleasant nonsense. We all know cads with beautiful faces. Lasting friendships are not based on what people look like or wear, but on what people are like inside, and how they behave as a result of their interior character. As my mother used to say, "Handsome is as handsome does."

In *The Body Project: An Intimate History of American Girls*, Joan Jacobs Brumberg of Cornell University addresses "The Jeaning Of America"—that is, the obsessive effort of today's teenage girls to get or keep slim—to avoid "thunder thighs"—even at the risk of their health. Pressured by diet and fashion ads, their preoccupation is with the shape of their bodies, rather than the shape of their minds. As teenagers might learn as they grow older, it is folly to agonize about our own exteriors, or to pick friends by what they look like, or what they wear. As Henry Thoreau warned in *Walden*, we should not think less of a man because he has a patch on his clothes. At Hanover I once sewed fake patches on my clothing, just to test the reaction. As time went on, colleagues were alternately amused, mystified, or irritated. Finally one faculty member accosted me and snapped, "Okay, what's the deal? Are you in a play, or what?"

Some people are turned off by looks, some by clothes, some by race. Even on college campuses, where prejudice still flares, some students are often surprised to learn that differences in skin color evolved by geographical accident. Some of our ancestors lived far away, and others closer to, the equator and therefore the sun's heat. Despite this scientific fact, civil rights legislation, the integration of schools, and the emergence of a minority middle class , many whites still have a hang-up on skin color—unless, of course, the individual wears a turban, a loin cloth, or is otherwise perceived as being "foreign." In fairness, it should be noted that every race has its own biases. According to Native

American legend, God "baked" man in an oven. On the first two attempts at creation, he under- and over-baked, thus producing the white and black races. Finally he got it right—a nice golden brown—and that was of course the Indian.

For many people, physical deformity is even more of a turn-off than skin color. Some years ago while I was at Hanover, I helped direct a camp for disabled children. When the first load of campers arrived at the beginning of the season, I was shaken. I had encountered only an occasional crippled child before, never a busload. Many of these youngsters had polio or muscular dystrophy, some were single or double amputees, two had elephantitis. The little girl who had no left forearm, only a small hand growing out of her elbow, affected me the most. Sickened by such physical deformity, I questioned my ability to do the job. But as I got to know the children over a period of weeks, something remarkable happened. The abnormalities began to disappear. Gradually, I saw only the *personalities* of children who yearned to be loved and nurtured as any child would. Their courageous spirits and contagious humor blinded me to their physical afflictions.

If I were teaching a course on "Love and Friendship," I would certainly refer to Machiavelli's famous guide for Renaissance rulers. As he saw it, we can tell the quality of a prince by the nature of his counselors. Similarly, we can tell the character of a person by the friends he selects. When we choose only friends who are like ourselves in social status, vocation, interests, and viewpoints, we are saying in effect that we don't want to broaden our horizons. Cicero was wrong when he said long ago that "friendship means a complete accord on all subjects, human and divine." To be sure, there must be some kind of bond to cement any friendship. Most of my friends, male and female, young and old, do not share my profession, my religion, or even my outlook on national and world affairs. Some of them are not even part of my generation. The bond that cements us for the most part is a common desire to serve the community and to help reduce human suffering at home or abroad. We agree on these ends, even while debating the means. In the process of such debates, we find ourselves tempering our own views as we listen to other perspectives from people we trust, our friends.

The disadvantage of "like me" friendships is that everyone reinforces each other's views, prejudices, and errors. Such arrangements may be comforting in the short run, but over time they tend to be boring, because no one is challenged to think differently. For that reason, many colleges commendably urge residential students to live for at least a year with a colleague from another country, religion, or ethnic group. This kind of experience is especially rewarding if conducted in another country, through a "Study Abroad" program. The new perspectives learned through such experiences transcend anything learned in the classroom. The resulting cross-cultural friendships often last for a lifetime.

Even more so than through arts or sports, true friends help channel our emotions in constructive directions, teach us views we might otherwise overlook, and most importantly of all, tell us the truth about ourselves when no one else will. Moreover, friends working together sometimes inspire each other, and often achieve more than they could accomplish individually. In London in the 16th Century, there was such a group of friends. They did not have the advantage of studying together in a single college where their efforts could be coordinated, nor did they have access to the computers and libraries that our students have today. But by exchanging ideas, they inspired one another. The result was that Christopher Marlowe, Ben Jonson, and of course Shakespeare produced a body of literature which will live forever.

Same gender friendship, like that in Shakespeare's day, is exhibited differently in different countries. In the United States, it can be as little as sitting quietly together on a park bench, or as much as a firm hand clasp. Even an arm around the neck is acceptable, especially if done playfully. In still-Puritan America, however, kissing is traditionally reserved for love between the sexes. Not so elsewhere. French and Russian men hug and kiss each other effusively, without the slightest self-consciousness, embarrassment, or hint of impropriety. Whenever I visit my male Greek friends, they leap to embrace and kiss me, as if I were a long lost member of their clan.

In Latin America, women even kiss men they have just met. When I was president of the University of Bridgeport, we had an academic center in Puerto Rico for teachers who sought a master's degree in Education. Each February I was asked to conduct the graduation ceremony. On the first such occasion, as the first young woman crossed the platform, I gave her the diploma with one hand, and the standard handshake with the other. She was visibly distressed. Looking at me plaintively, she said, "You not kiss?" Somewhat startled, I said, "Well, sure I kiss." Thirty-seven kisses later, I was beginning to think that a college presidency might be a pleasant experience after all.

Over the years students have asked me at times how to make lasting friendships. I usually confine my response to two tips. First, be patient. Don't judge a person too quickly; first impressions are often false. Good people, like good books, may seem dull at first, but they improve with time. We often deprive ourselves of what could be an inspiring friendship by leaping too soon to a negative conclusion about a new acquaintance. Secondly, show appreciation. It costs nothing, goes a long way toward cementing a relationship, and very often is rewarded with a positive response in return. When I completed a book on St. Thomas More at Harvard, I went on my own to thank President Nathan Pusey. Standing before his desk I said, "Dr. Pusey, I have just finished writing a book here at Harvard. Your librarians and professors have been most helpful, and I just wanted to say thank you." Pusey looked at me warily and asked, "And? What else?" "That's all sir," I said. "You mean," he said incredulously, "you have no complaint of any kind?" "No sir," I replied, "no complaint. Just thank you."

Pusey's reaction was startling. Muttering "Good heavens" to himself, he invited me to sit down, grabbed a 3 x 5 card and proceeded to write out my name and address. Suddenly he was telling me the problems he was having with faculty, what books he was currently reading, and even the location of his favorite mountain hideaway. Conscious of time and remembering his secretary's admonition, "You have fifteen minutes," I made several attempts to leave. But he kept saying, "No, no, sit down. I'm enjoying this." It was not until years later, when I too was a university president, that I realized how much an occasional pat on the back can mean. Pusey's establishment of a friendly intimacy with a young stranger was evoked by the simplest of gestures: an honest and heartfelt thank you.

If I were teaching a course on "Love and Friendship" I would end this part with one note of warning: beware of false friends. Thomas Paine, writing during the American Revolution, warned his readers against "sunshine patriots and summer soldiers" who suddenly appear when things are going well. Similarly, we must be wary of new "friends" who want to jump on the bandwagon once it's rolling. Remember Robert Manry (Chapter 2), who crossed an ocean in his homemade sailboat and was greeted by 40,000 Britons when he reached land? Manry appreciated the reception, but wanted most of all to return to the three friends who had seen him off at Cape Cod. They were the ones, he said, who were there when he needed them.

8

Education and Love

"Well fellows, are you ready for Sex as a Sacrament?"

I N MY COURSE ON "Love and Friend-ship," I would begin the "Love" part by discussing some of the philosophers and psychologists who have agonized over the nature of "romantic" love. Plato, for example, viewed love as the emotion produced by seeing Ideal Beauty embodied in a human form. Ernest Hemingway had a simpler and more profound definition. In *Farewell to Arms*, a priest says to Lt. Fred Henry, "Love is the desire to do things *for*." The priest was right. Love is giving, not getting. Love is "doing for," even when it is inconvenient or arduous, and we had planned to do something else. In the beautiful words of First Corinthians 13, "love does not insist on its own way." Few lovers consistently measure up to this definition.

A few Februaries ago, Ginny did not give me a Valentine's Day card. Instead, she took me to a lecture on love by a team of male and female psychologists. Their main point was that love is an *investment* of one's emotions, mind, and life in the life of another. Investments, of course, carry a risk, whether love, stocks, or real estate. One risk in loving is that one or both partners will lack the self-respect and personal security to maintain the relationship for long. To love, or to be loved, we must view ourselves as worthy. Don Meredith, the all-Pro Dallas Cowboy quarterback, once mesmerized an Alfred audience by explaining why he had lost his girl friend. "In *The City of God,* St. Augustine commands each of us to 'Love thyself,'" Meredith said. "I didn't love myself. How could I expect anyone to love me?"

One of the most difficult issues for today's students is the relation of sex to love. As a young professor at Hanover College, I was invited to dinner at the Phi Delta Theta fraternity house during Religious Emphasis Week. The understanding was that I would speak afterwards on the subject of "Sex as a Sacrament." The topic had been chosen by Phi Delts as a happy compromise between their interests and those of the Presbyterian institution. Unfortunately, I got my Greek letters confused, and wound up at Beta Theta Pi. The "wrong" brothers, out front playing softball, were dumbfounded when I arrived. The game ended abruptly as everyone raced inside for ties and jackets, one student whispering frantically, "Who invited *him?*" The members managed a half-baked dinner, but the conversation seemed strained, and their hastily assembled choral group sang raggedly at dessert, as if they were unprepared. When a painful pause developed after coffee, I took matters into my own hands and said cheerfully, "Well, fellows, are you ready for Sex as a Sacrament?" If I had disrobed publicly, they could not have been more shocked.

What I had hoped to get across that evening to the "right" brothers, was that all our relations with others should be guided by respect for the worth and dignity of the individual. Just as a sacrament is an outward and visible symbol of something inner and spiritual, so our physical relations with others should be consistent with our inner and spiritual feelings—that is, with our conscience. In sex, we reveal more than our bodies. We reveal our capacity to care. Colleges concerned with cultivating the emotional side of students should be willing to endorse this view, even if they do not hold Religious Emphasis Weeks.

For many of us, college still provides an opportunity to make the two biggest decisions of our lives: what will be our profession, and who will be our mate. In the latter regard, I was lucky. I returned to Juniata College after two years in military service, five weeks late for the fall semester. The only chair I could find in a crowded "British Drama" classroom was next to a young woman named Virginia Geyer. She was a happy and friendly musician with a compassion for people. She lent me her lecture notes (weak), and I carried her cello (heavy). For our first date, I suggested we go to Roundtop, a hill near campus, to look at the stars. She was understandably suspicious of this approach. But when we reached the hill, she was surprised (even secretly disappointed?) at what happened. I pointed out the various constellations and gave her a lecture on their relevance to navigation. That was it. Not even any hand-holding. After that somewhat uncertain start, one thing led to another, so to speak. Many years after that first date on Roundtop, and after many years of marriage, Ginny says I'm still on probation.

Literature is full of warnings about marriage. George Bernard Shaw, in the Preface to his play *Getting Married*, once satirized the institution in these words: "When two people are under the influence of the most violent, insane, delusive, and transient of passions, they are required to solemnly swear that they will remain in that excited, abnormal, and exhausting condition continuously until death do them part." Writing morosely on the same subject, the Columbia University professor Irwin Edman insisted that most couples "live a lifetime in the choking ashes of a brief remembered fire. [No wonder] most marriages wind up in resigned infelicity or rebellious infidelity."

Following the lead of Shaw and Edman, many counselors, therapists, academics, and popular authors have in recent years engaged in a frenzy of marriage bashing. Note, for example, *Closed Hearts, Closed Minds*, a recent report from the Council on Families under the auspices of the Institute for American Values. This study analyzes twenty textbooks used to teach marriage and family in 8,000 college courses. The report concludes that these texts offer "a determinedly bleak view of marriage" as "more of a problem than a solution." Only a few texts focus on the enormous evidence that children in single-parent homes are far more at risk than children in two-parent homes. Half of the books proclaim the early feminist view that marriage hurts women because it is an inherently oppressive institution. Yet Robert H. and Jeanette C. Lauer, in *Marriage and the Family: The Quest for Intimacy*, refer to 130 studies which show that "the tendency for married people to be happier and healthier is long-standing." The authors also cite a Gallup Poll showing that for 95 percent of Americans, family life is "very important"—in fact, much more important than work or religion. As John Leo says in a September '97 *U.S. News and World Report*, "the battle for public opinion may be over, but the losers are still writing the textbooks."

A common saying among psychologists is that couples who laugh together stay together. Witness one such couple, Matthew and Margaret Hill of the state of Washington. On their 50th wedding anniversary, Chief Justice Hill of the Washington Supreme Court was interviewed on television. "Judge," asked the interviewer, "to what do you attribute such a long and happy marriage?" "Well," said the judge, "it's quite simple. When Margaret and I got married, we agreed on a division of labor: I would handle the major problems, and she would handle the minor ones." "Wonderful," said the interviewer. "How has the formula worked out over the years?" "Beautifully," said the judge. "You see, there never have been any *major* problems."

Judge Hill is right, with one qualification. There will be no *major* problem in marriage if the two people entering the arrangement recognize that, as different sexes, they are *innately different* in personality, no matter how much they might think they are compatible. In recent decades, the more extreme feminists have clouded this critical difference. Some years ago, I gave a farewell reception for a young woman who was leaving my office for another position at UB. In the course of commenting on her many virtues, I especially noted how "vivacious" she had been despite the difficulties encountered in several supporting roles. At the end of my comments, a woman on the business college faculty confronted me. She was obviously upset about something. "Tell me," she said sharply, "do you use the word 'vivacious' for men?" "I've never really thought about it before," I replied. "Well," she snapped, "if you don't use the word for men, you shouldn't use it for women."

Her attitude reflects the worst features of early feminism, which denied any significant personality differences between men and women. Fortunately, what is "politically correct" is often factually wrong. As John Gray has documented in *Men Are From Mars, Women Are From Venus*, the two sexes think differently, communicate differently, and have very different views of what is important, especially in marriage. For the husband, the most important daily event might be an argument with the boss. But for the wife, unless she too works full time, the boss is irrelevant. Far more important to her is the fact that the sink leaks, or the garbage needs taking out, or the baby is spitting up.

The reader might argue that the differences described here are explained by different *roles*, not by inherent differences in personality or thought process. But in fact, men and women react differently even when involved in the same issue or event. Imagine, for example, a couple viewing a football game. The man will be furious that the Giants lost, because he's victory oriented. Simultaneously, the woman will wonder how the Lions' quarterback will get along with his wife, after being on the road for two weeks. Imagine further that the husband is doing the housework, and the wife is supporting the family. You can be sure, given this role reversal, that the man will give housework a much higher priority than previously. He will approach the leaking sink as an engineering problem to be solved, rather than as a disaster that precipitates an emotional torrent of despair.

Further evidence that men and women are essentially different, regardless of roles, was established by the Royal Society of Arts, which in March 1997 sponsored three London sessions tactfully entitled the "Eve and Adam Series." These "conversations" brought together people from politics, journalism, psychology, and gender studies to discuss the problems that men and women have in communicating with each other. The last of these sessions, on "Eden Revisited," was especially noteworthy for producing therapeutic hilarity for both genders. A male participant led off with this protest: "A man thinks that as long as he's said to a woman sometime within the last ten years that he loves her, that's enough—whereas women feel the need for this statement to be repeated again and again." There was also laughter and applause on both sides of the gender divide when another participant, this time female, wondered whether we can ever solve the communication problem, given that men and women use the same words to mean very different things. "Women use 'feeling' to describe their emotions," she said, "while men 'feel' merely hot, cold, tired, or hungry." As noted in Chapter 4, much the same points are made by Deborah Tannen in her book, *You Just Don't Understand.*

In the last analysis, a good marriage is a grand compromise. Each side wins some, loses some. Each partner is willing, on occasion, to be outvoted one to one. Both partners give a little, give up a little, forgive a little, and eventually make up a whole that is greater than the sum of its parts. In our high-powered era of rapid change, few spouses have the patience to finesse conflict this way. It follows that in modern society, any marriage that lasts more than ten years must be counted a miracle. At the last student session held in my home, as I retired from the UB presidency, a student asked if I would mind a personal question. "I guess not,"

I replied nervously. "Well," he said. "A lot of us would like to know, how long have you been married?" "That *is* a personal question," I said, "but I'm happy to answer it—forty years." The student fell silent for a moment, then smiled and said, "Okay Doctor, we'll buy the forty years. But with how many women?"

When Ginny and I first met, colleges—especially small ones—were jokingly referred to as "marriage factories," and with some justification. Uniformly, young people of both sexes, their hormones astir, shared the same place, work, and play for the same four-year time period. No wonder such a high proportion met their mates on campus. But times have changed. Today, many students are older part-timers who are already married, while many traditional undergraduates are marrying later and meeting their mates after campus days. Nonetheless, given the high divorce rate in this country and the stress level that today's dual careers engender, it might make sense for colleges to urge younger students to elect "Marriage and the Family," a course normally required for sociology majors. Of course we would need to find a more balanced textbook than those described in the Council on Families report.

If no balanced text could be found, an alternative to "Marriage and The Family" might be an elective course on gender studies or on "Marriage in Literature." Come to think of it, the latter could be a lot of fun. Marriage pro and con is a persistent topic in novels, poems, and plays. Just for starters, note Flaubert's *Madame Bovary*, Ibsen's *Hedda Gabler*, Tennyson's *Idylls of the King* (the Arthur/ Lancelot/Guinevere triangle), Wickham's *Collected Poems*, and Barrie's *What Every Woman Knows*. Nobody better expresses the frustration of the married woman who wants a career than the modern British poet Anna Wickham. In her poems, she rebels against the distractions of homemaking, ridicules her husband's stupid generalities, and demands space to exercise her own talent: "Of you, masters, slaves in our poor eyes/Who most are moved by women's tricks and lies/We ask our freedom!"

J. M. Barrie's play, *What Every Woman Knows*, deals with the similar frustration of not being valued. The central figure is John Shand, a dull but earnest man, who somehow manages to rise to be Prime Minister of Britain. One thing that puzzles him throughout this rise is that the speeches he delivers never seem to be quite the same as the ones he prepares. Only at the end of the play does he learn that his wife Maggie has been secretly revising the speeches, inserting humorous touches, which have made him an appealing political figure. When Shand makes this discovery, he demands that Maggie leave him, because she's destroyed his self-confidence. But Maggie replies, "Am I really to go, John? Won't you please keep me on? Every man who is high up loves to think that he has done it all himself; and the wife smiles, and let's it go at that. It's our only joke, John. It's just what every woman knows."

A broad education, with its exposure to history, literature, and psychology, can contribute to students' understanding of human relationships, teach them to distinguish myth from reality, and may even help guide them in their own personal marital choices. In any event, there are colleges that take seriously the need to develop and channel the emotional side of their students, and especially in this post-feminist age, to improve the attitude of men and women towards each other. For those who wish to initiate or expand upon such efforts, this chapter and the preceding one are offered as modest starting points.

9

Discovering Great Books

After the performance one little boy asked, "Mama, Is Shakespeare black?"

As NOTED IN PRIOR pages, the themes of friendship, love, and marriage are the substance of many, if not most, classics or great books. So what is a classic, anyway? The best definition I ever heard came from Holden Caulfield, teenage hero of Salinger's *Catcher in the Rye*. Holden said a classic is a book that, when you get done reading it, you wish the author was a personal friend of yours, and you could call him on the phone and talk to him about the problems of life.

Classics like *Catcher in the Rye* and *What Every Woman Knows* have a peculiar habit. They keep hanging around and appealing to large numbers of people, in many different countries, long after the time they were published. Thus a classic must be an "old" book. That means that a current book can't be a classic, and vice versa. To call a current work a classic, as some literary critics persist in doing, is like calling a horse the winner of the Kentucky Derby, just because he breaks well from the starting gate. Lots of horses break well and finish last. By contrast, a classic is a work that often gets off to a poor start. At the first turn it is breathing dust as it trails the pack. But this special kind of horse makes a courageous stretch run, and somehow gets its nose out in front by the literary finish line.

To dismount from my metaphor, what I'm trying to say is that classics don't depend for their ultimate fame on the initial reactions to them. Note Walt Whitman's *Leaves of Grass*, which begins with the famous poem, "Song of Myself." Today this volume is recognized as one of the great poetic achievements of American literature. It's been translated into many languages, and admired almost everywhere, especially in Italy and Latin America. But it was not always so. When *Leaves* was first published in 1855, it was ridiculed as the work of a madman. John Greenleaf Whittier was so shocked he threw his copy into the fire. There was only one good review of the book, which began with the stirring exclamation, "All hail, you American bard at last." As recent scholars have discovered, Whitman wrote the review himself!

Edgar Allan Poe's work is probably the most bizarre case in point. His collected poems never sold a single copy during his lifetime. But times change. Not long ago, a woman bought a bean pot for seventy-five cents at a New England auction. When she got home she discovered, wadded and wrinkled in the bottom, a booklet entitled *Poems by a Bostonian*. The "Bostonian" was Poe, and the "Poems" were the collected edition that didn't sell until Poe died. The woman sold her copy for $11,000. Immediately there was a frantic run on New England bean pots. Everybody wanted one. At a similar auction, another woman bought a similar pot, this time for $5.00. Lo and behold, at the bottom was another copy of you know what. She sold it for $32,000. Poor Poe would have been astounded.

When I think of the bean pot story, I think, not altogether seriously, of Miles's Law, which says, "The fame of a book often lies in reverse ratio to its initial reception." Translated that means, if a book is ridiculed and rejected on publication, it stands a good chance of achieving fame—witness James Joyce's *Dubliners*, Turgenev's *Fathers & Sons*, Edith Sitwell's poems, and don't forget Lincoln's *Gettysburg Address*. All of these works were scorned and deplored in their own time. The whole edition of *Dubliners* was burned in the streets of Dublin; and Sitwell, in the first public reading of her work, was chased out the back door of the auditorium.

At the opposite pole, of course, it is possible to cite many books that were lavishly praised at the outset, and are now utterly forgotten. Take Thomas Moore's *Lalla Rookh*, the romantic tale of a princess who fell in love with a troubadour, and then discovered he was her betrothed in disguise. The 19th Century public went crazy over this story, and its author. When Moore entered a theater in London, the play stopped and everybody applauded—even the actors. When he crossed the Irish Sea, five ladies broke into his cabin and kissed him while he struggled (probably not too hard) to escape. For many years, *Lalla Rookh* was one of the three books most read by Englishmen. The other two were Bunyan's *Pilgrim's Progress* and the Bible. But where is *Lalla Rookh* now? Dead and gone like its author.

When we consider books like *Leaves of Grass* (ridiculed but now a classic) and *Lalla Rookh* (praised but now forgotten), we are prompted to ask a crucial question: What are the qualities which make a classic durable, which permit it to wear well, which give it the capacity, in Milton's words, to "defy the tooth of time?" One such quality is certainly magical artistry. A prime example is "Stopping By Woods on a Snowy Evening." This poem makes us see and hear the snow falling as Robert Frost pauses in a neighbor's field to savor the soothing quiet of a winter night. Frost's images, subtle rimes, implicit symbolism, and plain words combine to produce his own unique idiom, so that we would know that he was speaking even if there were no title page. For different reasons, the same applies to A.E. Houseman, Carl Sandburg, and Virginia Woolf, whose *Mrs. Dalloway* reveals the thought and action of a married woman during a single day in London.

Another quality of classics is emotional power. A great book or poem hits us like a Mack truck, leaving a permanent scar on our souls. Our emotions can be roused by satire, as with Rabelais, Voltaire, and Swift; or by compassion, as with Galsworthy, *King Lear*, and Burns' "To a Mouse"; or by poignancy, as with the love sonnets of Elizabeth Barrett and Edna St. Vincent Millay. I think especially of Barrett's "If thou must love me," a fourteen line lesson on how *not* to love a woman; and Millay's "I know I am but summer to your heart/ And not the full four seasons of the year." In whatever form, the emotional impact of a classic is tremendous—which is why, once we've read a great work, we have trouble forgetting it. It becomes part of our thinking and behavior, even if on the subconscious level. No one who has read Cervantes' *Don Quixote* will ever forget the pathos of the old knight's death. Likewise for the final entry in Anne Frank's *Diary*, just a few days before the Green police discover her hiding place; or the final scene of Edmond Rostand's *Cyrano de Bergerac*, as Rosamund learns that the ugly Cyrano authored the eloquent letters that inspired her marriage to someone else.

Magical artistry and emotional power are important, but universal themes are probably the determining quality of a classic. A great book wrestles with some problem that has bothered men and women since Neanderthal days, and seeks to offer some tentative solution to that problem. Thus in *Billy Budd*, Melville asks, "Can there be any spiritual victory within physical defeat?" Hawthorne's *Scarlet Letter* raises an equally complex issue: Can sinning make a better person? (Let's hope so!) And D.H. Lawrence's *Sons and Lovers* poses a major issue for families: How much should parents seek to control the love lives of their children?

Over time, I've been on both sides of this last issue. When I was a young Air Force officer in Virginia, I fell in love, or thought I did, with a Southern girl. We planned the wedding for the Langley Field Chapel, and her mother sent out invitations. There was only one catch. According to Virginia law, I was underage, and needed my parents' consent. So I flew home with a light heart, not expecting any problem. Unfortunately, unbeknown to me, one of the invitations had been sent to my parents. By the time I arrived, they were apoplectic. "No!" my father yelled as I opened the front door. "What do you mean, 'no?'" I said. "You don't even know why I'm home." "Oh yes I do," my father replied in an agitated tremolo. "And the answer is no." By this time my mother had joined us, and I was furious. "Fascists!" I screamed. "Both of you are fascists!" (I had just learned the word in an orientation lecture, and this was my first opportunity to use it.) Now, as a parent myself, I feel that a little fascism never hurt anybody.

To be fair, college faculty should emphasize that everything said about literary classics also applies to great art, theater, and music, and to great works in history, science, and philosophy. Initial failure? Note Van Gogh, who left behind hundreds of paintings nobody wanted. Magical artistry? Check out Monet's *Water Lilies* and Renoir's *Boating Party*. Emotional power? Listen to any of the music composed by Tchaikovsky and Rachmaninov. Universal themes? What about de Tocqueville's *Democracy in America,* Gibbon's *Decline and Fall of the Roman Empire,* Darwin's *Voyage of the Beagle,* Marx's *Communist Manifesto.* The last work, along with F. Scott Fitzgerald's *The Great Gatsby,* was recently selected by sophomores at the University of California at Berkeley for pre-freshmen summer reading.

Many high school and college students are "turned off" by classics, often because they never had any parental or teacher encouragement during childhood. Such students, asked to read great books, often turn instead to *Cliff Notes*. Unfortunately, this and similar "study guides" contain none of the depth and flavor of the originals they attempt to summarize. The result is that students cheat themselves. They accept dishwater for wine. In my own reading experience, few classics have been really dull, but the teaching of them might be. Taught with verve and read with care, a single classic can be a joyful adventure all by itself, not once but on many re-readings. Classics are like good friends. They wear well.

One way to attract students to classics is to dispel generally held misconceptions. The first is that classics must be a century old. A generation (thirty years) of survival should be sufficient to qualify. Among recent or potential classics would be the novels of Toni Morrison, the works of the scientists Carl Sagan and Loren Eiseley, and much of the music of George Gershwin, Bob Dylan, and Simon & Garfunkel. If someone wants to add the Beatles, okay. They're old enough now, and I've mellowed.

Another misconception is that classics are "academic," and therefore remote from daily living. But in fact, great books surround us everywhere, every day. For this fact we can unexpectedly thank television. Luckily for us, this hungry monster has devoured quiz shows, soap operas, and comedians at such a frightful rate that producers and script writers now find themselves desperately dragging out, from the bottom of the barrel as it were, such semi-acceptable second-rate stuff as Homer's *Odyssey*, Melville's *Billy Budd*, and Faulkner's *The Sound and the Fury*. Even more amazing, the owners of mall-based movie houses are raking in profits from Hollywood versions of the Brontë sisters' *Jane Eyre* and *Wuthering Heights*; from Shakespeare's *Richard III*, *Romeo and Juliet*, and *Much Ado About Nothing*; and from Jane Austen's supposedly musty, prudish Victorian novels: *Emma*, *Persuasion*, and *Pride and Prejudice*. As for musical classics, they frequently comprise the sound tracks of TV programs, Disney animated cartoons, Lexus advertisements, and commercial films, even when the public is unaware of the source of the music. One of the most surprising box-office successes was *Babe*, a film about a talking pig who thought he was a sheepdog. The hilarity of the action was enhanced by appropriate classical music accompanying the barnyard scenes.

A third misconception about great books is that the roster or "canon" is fixed. This idea was exploded in 1988 when the Stanford University faculty met to debate whether the traditional canon of Western classics, used throughout the liberal arts curriculum, should be eliminated or reduced in favor of modern texts by feminists and minority writers. In effect this proposal suggested that Plato, Sophocles, Erasmus, John Locke, Rousseau, St. Luke, and Pasternak, for example, give way to "alternative writers" like Richard Wright, James Baldwin, Langston Hughes, Toni Morrison, and Maya Angelou. Those who favored this proposal argued that Plato and company were "dead white males" whose views were irrelevant for modern women and minorities, and therefore of no use in creating the intellectual "diversity" required of modern curricula. Those who opposed the proposal argued that, white male or not, the traditional canon was universal in values, it was required for any understanding of our Western heritage; and in any event, most feminist and ethnic literature had not survived long enough to qualify for "canonization."

Within months of the Stanford debate, similar controversies broke out on campuses throughout the country, culminating in an all-out war by the January 1989 meeting of the American Council on Education in San Diego. At that meeting, arguing in favor of altering the traditional canon, Marilyn Boxer, now Academic Vice President at San Francisco State, threw down the gauntlet. "A university is not a museum," she said. "It is a living institution that, like all living things, must constantly renew itself to survive." Thus was born such terms as "The Great Canon Controversy," and "The Multi-Cultural Wars." These "wars" were an extension of, and precipitated by, the "Politically Correct" debate that had earlier emerged.

In the last few years, tempers have cooled and wiser heads have prevailed on both sides. For many faculty, the issue is no longer "either/or." As early as November of 1989, Donald Rothman, a black professor at the University of California at Santa Cruz, wrote to Herman Blake, black provost at Indiana/Purdue Universities at Indianapolis. "Instead of arguing for replacement of classics by modern ethnic writers," he stated, "let's ask how our reading of the classics can be shaped by our reading of these other works, and vice versa." Determined to practice what he preached, Professor Rothman now teaches Shakespeare's *The Tempest* in tandem with Aime Cesaire's *A Tempest*, an adaptation of the original play to Black Theater. He also tells the story of a black mother who took her children to see a performance of Cesaire's version of

Shakespeare. After the performance, one little boy asked, "Mama, is Shakespeare black?" "Not yet," she replied.

Although the centerpiece of the Multi-Cultural Wars was older white males versus younger ethnics and women, a related issue was the relative merit of Western versus Eastern texts, given the increasing interdependence of countries and peoples worldwide. What many people argued then has now come to pass. The canon has been broadened to include classics from Asia and Third World countries. Teaching such works in tandem with similar Western classics is enlightening, because such comparisons highlight both the similarities and the differences between cultures. For example, *The Dream of the Red Chamber* by Tsao Chan (1792), is the story of the rise and decline of a great family—a favorite theme of Anton Chekhov (as in *The Cherry Orchard*) and other Russian writers. The most admired Japanese classic is *The Tale of Genji* (11th Century), written by a court lady, Murasaki Shikibu. Despite its age, *Genji* anticipates such modern themes as the anti-hero and the quest for a lost parent.

The rebellion against the "Western canon" capsized most traditional Great Books programs during the early 1990's. As we cross over to the 21st Century, however, such programs are roaring back at many institutions like Bethel (Minnesota), California Poly, Clemson, Louisiana State, and Middle Tennessee. These programs range from single courses to minors to on-line master's degree offerings. Some of the offerings include non-Western classics. But many Great Books directors are now declining to include books solely on the basis of ideology, race, or gender, suggesting that such works are more appropriate to courses in history, sociology, or political science. I agree. So, as in most other things, the pendulum is beginning to swing back, at least part way.

Colleges should teach students to respect classics, whether from East or West, not because they are old, but because they have survived. But a legitimate question remains. In an age of television, Web sites, virtual casinos, and professional football, why should anyone take time to *read* such books now? What claim to our attention do these works have, as they come clomping toward us out of the past? Their claim is that they keep us human. If we give them a chance, they help us develop imaginative compassion, psychological insight, and moral judgment. By the first, I mean the capacity to put ourselves in other peoples' shoes, and sympathize with problems as *they* see them. By the next, I mean the capacity to detect and adjust to our own inner self, and to the fluctuating interrelationships among individuals. By the last, I mean the capacity to determine not only the ethically best path in a given situation, but also to distinguish between our own impulses toward self-aggrandizement and the more altruistic messages coming from our consciences.

Through great books, we can develop and strengthen these distinctly human qualities. St. John's College in Maryland so much believes this, that they have made Great Books their entire curriculum. And for good reason. How read Dante's *Inferno* or Alan Paton's *Cry the Beloved Country* without having both our imagination and our compassion stretched? How read Thomas Wolfe's *Look Homeward Angel* or Dostoevsky's *Crime and Punishment* without enhancing our awareness of how humans interact with one another? How read Emily Dickinson without learning things we always suspected about ourselves? How read Thomas Hardy's *Tess of the D'Urbervilles* without rethinking our ethical codes so that we are more careful henceforth with words like "innocence" and "purity"?

The same applies to drama and fine arts. Henry Moore's sculptures and Picasso's abstracts stimulate our imagination, in the same way that watching Puccini's *Madame Butterfly* deepens our compassion. As for psychological insight, an Alcoa vice president once told me that he learned more from *Hamlet* than from any psychology text. Some years ago I saw Vivian Leigh and John Gielgud in *Ivanov*, a Chekhov play about a Hamlet-like man who is disintegrating physically, mentally and spiritually, because he regards himself as a failure. No one can see this play without realizing the terror and loneliness of failure, and without conceding that there is a bit of failure in all of us. From great art, opera, and drama, we often learn more about our own psyche than we really want to know.

Great works also help us to sharpen our moral codes. One of the most relevant plays here is John Osborne's *Inadmissable Evidence*. It is the story of a lawyer who has always leaned on friends, sought nothing but monetary success, and worshiped sex while ignoring love. We cannot witness this tragedy without realizing that an acceptable scale of values is the reverse of that practiced by this unfortunate protagonist. The same applies to Goethe's *Faust*, in which a scholar sells his soul to the devil for temporary self-fulfillment.

Human beings at their best share the qualities of imaginative compassion, psychological insight, and moral judgment. Machines, even at their best, do not. These differences between humans and machines are worth preserving. That's why educated people continue to cherish the classics —to read the books, attend the plays, visit the museums, support the symphony orchestras. *Such works help maintain and nourish those human qualities that distinguish us from machines in a machine age.* Seen from this perspective, a love of classics is one of the most important attributes that a college can bestow upon students, as they move from their campus sanctuary to the technology-driven society that exists beyond.

10

Coping With Change

A roto-press has broken loose from its moorings, invaded the Capitol, and painted "Fiddle-dee-dee" in three-color process all over Senator Sloop's backside.

ONE OF THE CHIEF functions of college is to help students prepare for change, especially for the startling technological changes that are occurring as we enter the 21st Century. Most of us have difficulty coping with change, and many of us tend to "cope" by simply resisting.

I have been resisting some modern art for years. What first turned me off was a news story in the *Cincinnati Inquirer*. It seems that "Charlie," a gorilla in the city's zoo, had been given a paint box by his trainers. It was supposed to be a joke, but things got out of hand. Gleeful with his new toy, Charlie swiftly produced dozens of oddly colored "abstracts" which began out-selling the local artists. Alarmed at this unfair competition, the artists demanded that the art spree be halted. Can you imagine Holbein or Velasquez being worried about competing with an ape?

In academic galleries and museums, I have seen my fill of stomped-upon bugles, broken neon tubes, and multi-colored paper towels hung from strings at different levels. Even if this is serious art, will it survive? Don't get me wrong. I like some of De Kooning's work, own some abstract paintings, and once lunched with Robert Motherwell of "ink blot" fame. We discussed a painting that had just won first prize at the Detroit Art Museum. It was wholly black, marred only by a single white dot in the upper right hand corner. Motherwell argued that it was a masterpiece of simplicity, noting that two dots would have made the painting "too busy."

Ginny has had her own problems with change. As a classical musician, she was never too comfortable with the rock and roll stuff. Glenn Miller and the swing bands were great, but not rock and roll. So she got some UB students together and told them, "What we need around here is a formal dinner dance." They liked the idea, and "Winter Prelude" was born. There were white tablecloths, candlelight, evening gowns, corsages, three-piece suits. I didn't recognize half the students! But to Ginny's consternation, they *still* had a rock and roll group. To make matters worse, they seated us at the table of honor—right in front of the amplifiers. The student planning committee came to her afterwards, quite proud of their work, and asked for a critique. Ginny said, "Everything was beautiful, except for one thing." "What's that?" they asked. "Well," she said, "At a formal dance you have an orchestra like Peter Duchin's. You don't have a rock and roll group." "Why not?" they responded. That had her stumped. Later they came to her with a compromise proposal. "Look," they said. "We like rock music, but you don't. So here are two sets of ear plugs for you and the president." It was a solution worthy of the United Nations.

My problem with rock and roll was not the music. "Tommy" by The Who was okay by me. My problem was the "no touch" dancing which accompanied the music. At a student dance held my last year as UB president, a girl asked me to dance, weaved and shook five yards away, and then suddenly disappeared. There I was, jiggling and shimmying all by myself like an idiot, past midnight, with a couple hundred students yelling "Go, go, go!" Finally the band leader (sorry, "group" leader) stopped the musical mayhem and shouted, "I've noticed this older gentleman hanging in there all night. It's most admirable. Sir, would you please identify yourself?" Since he was the only one who didn't know who I was, there was a lot of laughter and wild applause.

Modern art and music are of course minor changes compared with the explosion of knowledge that characterizes the last half of the 20th Century. Four centuries earlier, during the Renaissance, Francis Bacon proclaimed that he "took all knowledge" for his province. Even as late as Thomas Jefferson and Ben Franklin in our own country, similar Baconian assertions were sometimes made and went without challenge. But today no intellectuals would be taken seriously if they so described the scope of their own knowledge. Anyone who claimed today to know everything about everything, or even everything about one field, would automatically be considered a candidate for the laughing academy.

Since I was born, television, penicillin, frozen foods, Xerox copiers, plastics, laser surgery, MRI's, CAT Scans, test tube babies, and contact lenses have become common knowledge; Scotch Tape and Frisbies are household words. As a child, my favorite Halloween story was of a witch who boasted that she could fly on a broomstick. A little boy countered, "That's nothing. Look at this," and turned on a water faucet. The witch blanched at the rush of water, and screamed "Earth magic!" If she was astonished at running water, what would her reaction be to the Hubbell telescope, the Columbia space probes, or the Mars Pathfinder?

A short time ago I was talking with Joseph Engelberger, father of the industrial robot. Thirty years ago, Americans ridiculed his gadget. Unfortunately for us, the Japanese thought it was a great idea. Joe was saying that computers have already replicated 75 percent of the human brain. Once they have reached 100 percent, he argued, they will have "being," because mind is being. The mind of a computer will then be just like ours—except that it will work faster. "But Joe," I protested. "What about compassion? What about love?" "Don't worry," he laughed. "We'll program that in."

I can never tell when Joe is kidding. Sometimes he just likes to start a good argument. What is unnerving, however, is that Joe is not the only one talking this way. Some scientists contend that human brains and computers are already more alike than anyone would have believed a few years ago. Each is a thinking machine, they say, that operates on little pulses of electricity traveling along wires. According to NASA scientist Robert Jastrow in *The Enchanted Loom*, scientists will soon be able to reproduce the total human mind within a machine, which will then possess life á la Engelberger, "because mind is the essence of being." Jastrow hails the coming era when "at last the human brain, ensconced in a computer, has been liberated from the weaknesses of the mortal flesh." He sees such computer minds as rapidly developing into ever higher forms of intelligence which will make the human brain as obsolete as the dinosaur. Jastrow's ultimate vision is of immortal self-aware robots exploring space in hopes of finding a new race of primitive innocents like ourselves.

Jastrow must be writing tongue-in-cheek? Surely he realizes that machines can never have life as humans experience it? But wait a minute. That's exactly what happens in Karl Capek's *R.U.R. (Rossum's Universal Robots)*. At the end of that play, two robots fall in love, get married, and reproduce. An equally bizarre scenario is presented in Stephen Vincent Benet's "Nightmare #4." In that remarkable poem, Benet escapes to the roof of his apartment house, where he watches in astonishment as machines launch a revolt against their masters. Streetcars chase policemen down the street, beauty shop hair dryers decapitate their customers, phone cords strangle startled secretaries, and a Cadillac rams two Wall Street brokers against the Racquet Club steps. As Benet listens in horror to his portable radio, he hears of other atrocities. A cement mixer in New Jersey has just swallowed a worker. And in Washington, a roto-press has broken loose from its moorings, invaded the Capitol, and printed "Fiddle-dee-dee" in three-color process all over Senator Sloop's backside.

Some critics will protest that Benet is personalizing machines, that he is giving technology a life of its own. But as we've learned from experience, technology sometimes seems to do just that, much like fictional characters sometimes develop their own momentum and escape the novelist's control. In John Galsworthy's *Forsythe Saga*, the author publicly claimed that his characters had developed their own lives, and he was no longer responsible for them!

Much the same thing seems to have happened in the recent arms race. As the weapons got larger and more dangerous, each side strove to one-up the other in a kind of global Russian roulette. One is reminded of an old Thai legend, replicated on so many Bangkok temples. The legend tells of birds that carried snakes away in their claws. So the snakes swallowed stones to make themselves too heavy to lift. In retaliation the birds picked up the snakes by their tails and shook them so that the stones fell out. Counter-measures by the snakes and counter-counter-measures by the birds accelerated with increasing ferocity. By the time this kind of process culminated in our real world, a combined nuclear arsenal of 12,000 megatons was held by the two superpowers. With that many warheads, the U.S. could obliterate every Soviet citizen three times over. The Russians could kill each of us seven times. This discrepancy in overkill was called "the missile gap." It was the type of logic that could have come out of *Alice in Wonderland.*

Poetic and fictitious accounts of technology run riot might be amusing to some but ominous to others, because the literary imagination has often foreshadowed actual events. The science fiction of writers like H.G. Wells, Jules Verne, and Isaac Asimov often becomes, within a relatively short time, scientific reality. But Engelberger and Jastrow notwithstanding, machines do not have minds now, and are not likely to have them in the future. Machines are constructed and manipulated, for better or worse, by human beings. It is not the technology itself, but its *use*, which requires monitoring. A case in point is the Internet, through which pedophiles prey on innocent children.

Particularly worrisome is the use of machines to invade our privacy, and even to substitute for some of our most sacred rituals. Software is now available whereby computers can match mates and even conduct weddings for folks too busy to worry about church services. Especially intrusive in our private lives are the unsolicited sales calls from telemarketers, using computerized data banks. These kinds of intrusions have become so pervasive that anti-telemarketing consultants and publications have emerged. A self-help book, *How to Get Rid of Telemarketers*, was recently published by Bad Dog Press of Roseville, Minnesota. Among the suggested turn-offs are the following: "I'm so glad you called. I've just broken up with my lover and am terribly lonely. Are you a Capricorn? You sound like a Capricorn. . . . What? . . . Hello? . . ." Or when an aggressive realtor calls, burst into tears and sob, "Is this some kind of joke? My house burned down last night and we lost everything."

Vince Nestico, a 25-year-old draftsman from Detroit, has created a Web site, The Anti-Telemarketer Source (www.izzy.net/vnestico/t.market.com). He offers a "Telemarketer Torture Tape," containing various responses that can be played into the phone when a telemarketer calls. In one response, a mellifluous male voice intones, "If you want to press one, press one. If you insist on pressing two, go ahead and press two. . . ." Among the suggested comebacks to unsolicited sales calls, culled from the Torture Tape, are the following: "Shhh. Wait a minute. I'm here robbing the house. Whoa! I think the owners just got back. Can you hold?" And this: "I'm sorry, but I'm busy right now. Give me your home number and I'll call you back tonight when *you* are at dinner. Hello? . . . Hello? . . ."

Despite Benet's poem, machines are not yet chasing policemen down the street. But if we wanted to be paranoid, we could suggest that they are beginning to crowd us, to hem us in, to press us to be *more like them*—or at least to default and admit our inferior status. Thus the *New York Times* on May 12, 1997, announced an unsettling development. "In brisk and brutal fashion, the IBM computer Deep Blue unseated humanity . . . yesterday, when Gary Kasparov, the world chess champion, resigned the sixth and final game of the match after 19 moves, saying, 'I lost my fighting spirit.' " Unseated humanity? Wow! Maybe we should re-read Jastrow.

Humanity will probably stay around for a while, but technology is clearly in the saddle; it pervades every aspect of modern society. It has even invaded the territory of its alleged archenemy, the humanities. The more fanatic engineers tell us that we no longer need artists, because computers can draw designs for us, even in color. Electronic music, they insist, will render Beethoven, or Mozart, or Brahms even more accurately than a renowned symphony orchestra. Moreover, electronic music is purer, more dependable, more accurate, and best of all, strike-free! Technology is even being applied to literary analysis. Scholars recently used computers to analyze Hamlet's character, identify Milton's influence on Shelley, and trace the spiritual growth of the Irish poet, William Butler Yeats.

Even I am a beneficiary of technology's earth magic. I compute budgets with a hand calculator, use a word processor to revise speeches, dictate memos into a micro-Dictaphone, receive E-mail via the Internet, send faxes to Moscow, and take the air shuttle to Washington and Boston. In fact, technology is so ubiquitous in everyday life that some people credit it with phenomena that are completely unrelated. While on a flight to Los Angeles not long ago, I sat next to an inquisitive older lady, who told me that this was her first airplane ride. When the pilot announced that we would arrive early, she turned and said, "Why do you think that is?" "We probably have a tail wind," I replied. "Isn't that nice," she said, and brightened immediately. "You know, they ought to have those on all the airplanes."

The advance of technology in the later 20th Century has had a devastating impact on enrollment in liberal arts programs. I am referring here to the arts, humanities, and social studies, as distinguished from the physical sciences and professional fields. In 1971 one half of all full-time undergraduates in the United States were in the liberal arts as just defined. By 1977, only one third were so designated. Since 1984, the number has been between 10 and 20 percent depending on gender. Most students in college today are majoring in such technical fields as pre-med or pre-dental science, business, engineering, nursing, industrial design, medical technology, information management, computer science, or the like. No wonder that some educators speak of "the eclipse of the liberal arts" and "the flight from the humanities." Typical of such talk is Alvin Kernan's recent book, *What's Happened to the Humanities?* It tells us that literature and company "are coming to be perceived as increasingly less relevant and less necessary to modern life than other forms of knowledge."

This trend is reflected in the composition of presidential cabinets. Increasingly, cabinet members have business, industrial, and technical backgrounds. We might argue that the government should be organized by English majors and run by graduates in philosophy. We might insist that the Congress would be more enlightened if composed of humanities and social science graduates. But such is not going to be the case any time soon. It is therefore imperative for democracy that the liberal arts continue to be part of the education of those who govern the country, as well as those who lead our corporations and engineering firms. After all, man cannot live by computers alone.

Under these circumstances, the liberal arts are more urgently needed than ever. For starters, they provide a sense of stability in a world that now moves with the speed of light. The Concorde arrives in London from New York in less than three hours, a FAX machine in New Delhi can send a memo to Pittsburgh in minutes, and cellular phones ruthlessly track us down like criminals no matter where we are. The new name of the game is instant communication. In 1988, a single fiber optic cable could carry 3000 messages. By the year 2100, a single fiber may carry as many as 10 million messages. This means that we will soon be able to transmit the entire *Encyclopedia Americana* from New York to London in one second! As one student recently said to me, "Man, we're really moving!" Yes, but where are we going, where are we headed, what's the goal, where is the time for reflection even to identify a goal? One thinks of Thoreau who said, "The man whose horse trots a mile a minute does not carry the most important messages."

Today the carousel of change is whirling so fast that some of us want to get off. Those who hang on are having trouble keeping their footing. In this world of incredible flux, movement, and speed, the humanities gives us a center, a stable platform on which to stand. Great literature like Thomas Hardy's *Mayor of Casterbridge* and John Keats' "Ode on a Grecian Urn" provide that stability because they are universal, they stay with us and grow better over time. Great books and renowned works of art and music are not subject to changes in computer models or new forms of telecommunication. Thus they give us a sense of permanence. They provide ballast that keeps us steady in a windy world of perpetual flux and flow.

Not only are we disoriented by speed, we are also assailed by a tidal wave of printouts. As John Naisbett tells us in *Megatrends*, information is doubling every twenty months. We struggle to keep up, and in the process *drown in data while starving for knowledge*. We are frustrated by a world that won't stand still, that seems to have the St. Vitus' Dance. What seems a certainty today turns out to be doubtful, different, or wrong tomorrow. The faster we move, the more life becomes a perpetual state of emergency, a kind of daily crisis management.

In such an environment, the arts and humanities can provide a spiritual reservoir, a cultural escape hatch, a calm amidst the vortex of the storm. Pablo Casals' cello, Verdi's soaring arias, or Toynbee's historical perspective can provide mental refreshment from the constant tensions, pressures, and strains that accompany our technological benefits. Many of us yearn to emulate Robert Browning's medieval organist, Abt Vogler, who lifted himself to God and peace through ever-ascending spirals of sacred music. It is no coincidence that in recent years doctors and therapists have discovered the healing powers of the arts, music, and poetry. In his recent book *The Mozart Effect*, Don Campbell describes how the power of music is being tapped to deal with anxiety, cancer, pain, and mental illness. The director of a coronary care unit in Baltimore is quoted as saying that a half hour of classical music has the same effect on his patients as 10 milligrams of Valium. Even more astounding, we are told that high school students who sing or play an instrument score up to fifty points higher than their peers on the SAT's.

Still another benefit of the arts and humanities as an adjunct to professional education is the flexibility it provides in addressing an ever-shifting job market. In our Age of Technology, jobs keep changing to meet new problems and needs. According to sociologists, the average American college graduate will change careers at least six times by age 65. Most of these jobs, for some of which we do not even know the function yet, will require multi-disciplinary training. The liberal arts provide the breadth necessary to adjust to these new opportunities. As Larry Schnack, chancellor of the University of Wisconsin at Eau Claire, recently said, "It is important that graduates know how to . . . incorporate broader areas of knowledge into their own specialities, so that . . . they will be flexible enough to adapt as their jobs change." These broader areas of knowledge also strengthen those qualities of mind, mentioned in Chapter 9, which distinguish us from machines in a machine age: imaginative compassion, psychological insight, and moral judgment. To those we can add others, especially communication and critical analysis.

These qualities constitute the "art of human relationships," which is of course essential to our success in the world beyond work—as mothers, fathers, neighbors, citizens. But this "art" is also the critical factor in career success, whether we are a corporate manager, public agency director, hospital administrator, chief of engineering, or whatever. How can we "get ahead" professionally if we cannot communicate, analyze, and imagine ourselves in others' shoes? If we cannot understand and sympathize with the feelings and concerns of our associates? If we cannot make decisions about them and the company which they see as fair? Without sensitivity to human beings, no vocational role can be performed effectively, and no technical decision will work. Professional success depends on an environment of human support, and professional decisions are sabotaged if people are not willing to implement them.

So where did this idea come from that the liberal arts are "impractical," that they are a pleasant asset for leisure time, but not terribly relevant for the workplace? In fact, the "art of human relationships" is pre-requisite to corporate or any other type of leadership. That's why "Fortune 500" executives flock to Colorado's Aspen Institute each summer to study classics from Thucydides to Norman Mailer. They certainly don't go for a vacation, because the mental and physical routine is harsh. They go so they can gain the inspiration, insight, and perspective necessary to make their companies more competitive, and therefore more profitable. How much more "practical" can you get?

Especially in an Age of Technology, every college is obligated to assure that its graduates can earn a decent living, regardless of undergraduate major. Meeting that obligation for the declining corps of liberal arts majors will require considerable ingenuity in the next decades. At a minimum, colleges should strive for computer literacy among all non-technical students. "Work oriented" minors should also be developed for students majoring in fields that lack entry-level opportunities. A student majoring in painting or sculpture might take a minor in industrial or graphic design, thus securing initial job protection while seeking to establish an artistic reputation. The co-op program of alternating classroom and work semesters, usually reserved for engineering and business students, should be opened to arts, humanities, and social science majors. This experience would give them an opportunity not only to test their job potential in a variety of occupations, but also to explore the relationship of their field to the workplace beyond college.

Most important of all, the ascendency of technology demands that we strengthen and expand the liberal arts core, i.e., the general education requirements for both technical and non-technical students. We cannot require non-technical students to be science majors, but we can require them to learn the chief problems, achievements, and failures of modern applied science. Similarly, we cannot require technical students to major in philosophy, but we can require them to learn the chief ideas in philosophical history. When I am in a commercial aircraft preparing to land, I don't much care whether the pilot is conversant with Plato. But if he has taken some philosophy or psychology or history in college, he will probably be a kinder captain for his crew, especially in emergencies, and a more interesting person for his family. As for the core generally, it should be at least a third of the total hours required for graduation; the required courses should be related to one another through a cohesive principle or integrative theme; and a senior capstone course, maybe "Coping with Change," should provide the opportunity for students of mixed academic backgrounds to focus all their prior learning on the issues raised in this and other chapters.

The function of the liberal arts, through such a required core, is not to substitute for the technical fields, but to enrich them; to humanize technology, to encourage imaginative management, and to create a compassionate and moral framework for professional decisions. This function is what a philosophy department chairman must have had in mind when I met him one day on campus. "My majors are now co-oping," he said, beaming. "What on earth can philosophy majors do in a business corporation?" I asked. "Anything, everything!" he shouted, as he rushed to class. As he entered the building, he stopped, turned around, waved, and yelled, "Besides, they can serve as the conscience of the company!"

11

Ethics and Technology

"You've got to let us lie a little, or we'll get our blocks knocked off!"

SOME PEOPLE WOULD scoff at the idea that a company should have a conscience. These are the same people who regard moral values as an impediment, a kind of monkey wrench in the machinery of life. I am reminded of a lengthy discussion that my UB Cabinet once held on a serious issue. At the end of the discussion there appeared to be agreement on how to proceed. At that point I asked a key question. "What would be the moral dimensions of this course of action?" One Vice President replied in exasperation, "There you go, Lee, muddying the waters again."

As irritating as it might be to others, we must sometimes "muddy the waters" if we want to maintain our personal integrity and the reputation of our organizations. In the university as in the corporate world, decision-makers are constantly whipsawed between expedience and morality. Sound decisions cannot be made outside of a moral framework. Without some kind of ethical code as an anchor, we are dragged away by the undertow. In Arthur Miller's *All My Sons*, a manufacturer knowingly ships defective engine heads to the Air Force during World War II. In a trick of fate, the flawed parts are installed in P-40 aircraft sent to his son Larry's squadron in China. A number of the planes crash and the pilots are killed. Larry learns of his father's crime, and fatally crashes his own plane in shame. The father belatedly realizes, in an outburst of grief and anguish, that in a moral sense all the young men were his sons, and he betrayed them for money.

The purpose of college is not to impose an "official" or preconceived scale of values on students, but to expose them to a wide range of ethical thinking so that they can develop their own value scales as guides in their post-commencement lives. For that purpose, it is imperative that the college as an institution be dynamically neutral, as described in Chapter 5. Institutional neutrality is pre-requisite to a free discussion and weighing of alternate values and their respective worth. It is also imperative that graduation requirements include an ethics course drawn from the great philosophies and religions, both East and West. Featured in such a course should be works like Plato's *Republic*, Thomas More's *Utopia*, and Francis Bacon's *New Atlantis*, which explore the nature of individual virtue and just societies. Also helpful in such a course would be the great anti-utopias like Orwell's *1984*, which terrifyingly depicts the reverse of virtue and justice.

This required ethics course should confront head-on the controversial field of "situational ethics." In setting forth his doctrine of the "Categorical Imperative," Immanuel Kant argued that lies corrupt the Moral Law of the universe. Therefore, he proclaimed, "I would not tell a lie to save 10,000 men." But anyone of us would lie immediately, if it were the only way to save the life of a loved one, or to protect fellow soldiers who would otherwise be destroyed.

When I was assistant director of Maryland's Camp Greentop for handicapped children, I developed a close relationship with Bernie Greenwalt, who had muscular dystrophy, considered then and now to be a fatal disease. At the end of the season, when his parents came to take him home, he asked to talk with me privately. We sat on the side of the pool, and he said, looking straight into my eyes, "Mr. Lee, am I ever going to get well?" I could not lie to him, but I could not tell him the whole truth either. So how did I respond? I told him that medical science was discovering new cures every day, so there was always room for hope. What I did not say was that in his case, the hope would need to be realized soon, if he was to be saved.

On a less dramatic level, all of us tell friends just out of the hospital how "great" they look. We want to boost their morale, even though doing so requires a "white lie." So when is lying wrong? It is wrong when we use it selfishly to advance ourselves, or callously to diminish human dignity, or hypocritically to avoid a commitment that we supposedly made in good faith. At the bottom of situational ethics there is still a core of absolute morality. Nothing intrigues students more than debating these matters, especially if real life case histories are used.

It is also wrong to lie to get one up on your opponent. At one point in collective bargaining at UB, the faculty went on strike, and put out a statement justifying their position. To speak charitably, the statement was not factual. At the next cabinet meeting, a vice president circulated his proposed rebuttal. It also was not factual. When I vetoed the rebuttal on those grounds, the officer slammed his fist on the table and blurted, "Lee, you've got to let us lie a little, or we'll get our blocks knocked off." But two lies do not make a truth. It is also stupid to lie in this kind of situation, because any misrepresentation is a potential boomerang. It is likely to be discovered, to the detriment of the party who originated it. In the long run, it is far more effective to identify the flaws in an opponent's argument.

In addition to the ethics course required of all students, modern colleges should require special ethics courses for business and engineering majors. For the former, a new type of course combining ethics and law with business practices should replace the traditional "Business Ethics," which was labeled "a joke" by MBA students meeting recently for their annual convention at the University of Virginia. Instead of mildewed theory, this new course would focus on case histories in the corporate world.

Such a course would involve critiquing codes of conduct developed by Fortune 500 companies like Pitney Bowes, General Electric, and AT&T; debating the difference between "illegal" and "unethical" as presented in such codes; reviewing news articles and court records on corruption and dishonesty at high corporate levels, especially in the tobacco industry; studying the new Federal Sentencing Guidelines, which encourage judges to get tough on white collar crime; analyzing the financial and other damage to companies whose executives have been convicted; identifying revisions in ethical codes resulting from such litigation; and coming to conclusions as to what kind of leadership, procedures, and corporate environment produces ethical conduct by all ranks of employees. A final term paper could require students to write their own codes of conduct for modern corporations, and in the process to explain why certain ethical principles were included or excluded.

In this special course for business students, special attention should be given to the problems faced by multi-national corporations which operate in countries where ethical standards differ from our own. While president of UB, I founded Tower Fellows, a group of Fortune 500 chief executives who met in the DuPont Tower Room atop one of our buildings. The first session of the Fellows dealt with corporate morality. Fred Allen, Board Chairman of Pitney Bowes, had launched the "corporate morality" movement before the American Chamber of Commerce in Zurich, Switzerland, in 1975. At the Tower Fellows meeting ten years later, he read from the core of that speech, which included this passage:

> Unethical corporate practices have a corrosive effect on free markets and free trade. They subvert the laws of supply and demand, and they short-circuit competition based on classical ideas of product quality, service, and price. Most importantly, these practices erode the base of public support and respect so necessary for the growth of the free market system.

Mr. Allen went on to quote from Franklin Roosevelt's Second Inaugural Address. "We have always known that heedless self-interest was bad morals; we know now that it is bad economics."

Using Fred Allen's views as a departure point, I followed with an academic (and in retrospect, pedantic) survey of absolutist ethics. When I finished, the first person to reply was Barclay Morley, CEO of Stauffer Chemical. He needed to get crucial equipment to a Stauffer factory in Mexico, he said. However, the shipment could not be delivered unless he paid an "expediting fee," otherwise known as a bribe. On the basis of his personal code of ethics, Morley was opposed to paying the fee. On the other hand, as CEO he recognized his responsibilities to his workers. If the shipment did not go through, the factory would close, and 600 people would lose their desperately needed jobs. So Morley turned to me and said, in front of all the others, "Now, Mr. President, what would you do under these circumstances?" "Let me think about that, Barc," I said weakly, playing for time. When I did think about it during the days following, I realized I would have done exactly what Morley did. To the extent possible, a CEO's duty is to his people, not himself.

Another special ethics course, for science and engineering students, would focus on live issues raised by modern technology, which has moved the moral frontier beyond the traditional province of philosophers. These issues involve three questions: What's the priority? Who makes the decision? Toward what objective? Concerning the first category, we could ask what's more important, to create jet aircraft which get to Paris in three hours, or to unclog the traffic in city streets across America? To create a pure life environment for spacecraft, or reduce the unhealthy pollution of our urban areas? To qualitatively improve our nuclear weaponry, or to fund peaceful atomic projects? To focus behavioral science on sexual conduct and psychoanalysis, or on diplomacy, dispute resolution, and peacemaking? The questions could be predicated on the assumption that funding was available for only one alternative in each pair.

Another cluster of issues raises different questions. Genetic engineers have already cloned mammals, and are prepared to clone human beings. Inspired by the ethical debate on this issue, Franklin and Marshall College recently selected Mary Shelly's *Frankenstein* for summer reading by incoming freshmen. The work asks a profound question. To what extent can science invade with impunity God's prerogative for creation? *Frankenstein* and ethical considerations aside, cloning of humans will almost surely take place in the next decade. Toward what objectives will this be done? Who is to make the decision?

Again, the molecular biologist can now modify the gene structure of existing organisms. With the Human Genome Project largely complete, we are now on the threshold of changing human physical characteristics, even to the extent of providing longer arms, or shorter legs. Do we wish to produce people with one eye? Two noses? Three ears? By whose standards of beauty, or utility will we do this? Who is to make such decisions, and toward what objectives? It is important that pre-med and similar undergraduates be made aware early on that when they start practicing their professions, they will be responsible for answering such questions and for acting in conformance with those answers. Given that scenario, a college would be irresponsible if it did not start giving them some guidance along the way.

Toward that end, this special course for science and engineering students could require majors to apply the principles learned in the general ethics course to modern technological issues like those described above. C.P. Snow has said, "Technology has two faces: one benign and one threatening." This special course could be aimed at answering the overriding question that Snow has indirectly posed: In the New Millennium, how can we control technology so that it enhances rather than diminishes our quality of life?

It might be that such a question cannot be answered until college curricula change. In much of our current higher education system, philosophy students are permitted to ignore technology, while science and engineering students are allowed to ignore philosophy. The result is that both types of students graduate lacking crucial knowledge the other has.

Worse still, many of our universities permit business, health, and social science students to avoid *both* philosophy and technology (aside from basic computer literacy). This further educational deficiency poses a special problem for society, because it is these kinds of students who frequently become our public policy makers. They are the ones who often become our corporation executives, elected officials, military chiefs, government agency directors, hospital administrators, and community leaders. Remember, these leaders have no education in philosophy or technology, yet they are called upon to make decisions on the location of nuclear plants, clean air regulation, genetic engineering opportunities, and the dismantlement of multiple warhead missiles. Considering their educational deprivation, we should not be surprised if their decisions are sometimes grounded in ignorance.

If this problem is to be resolved, we must start getting tough with our liberal arts core. All students, regardless of future career interests, must be introduced to ethical concepts from Plato to the modern relativists. And whether they want to or not, all students must be introduced to the history of technology, including pioneers like Leonardo da Vinci, the emergence of Silicon Valley as a national force, and future technological prospects both benign and threatening. A big step in the right direction would be to help students cross the bridge between ethics and technology by studying the philosophy of science, and by participating in seminars on moral issues posed by modern engineering genius.

C.P. Snow once claimed that "the only weapon we have against technology is technology itself." Maybe so. But a better weapon is an education that integrates science with the humanities, and especially technology with philosophy. When we have developed that kind of integrated curriculum, we might then be able to produce leaders who dare to question and evaluate progress. On occasion they may even dare to reject progress because it is not worth the price we must pay. Ralph Waldo Emerson once made the comment that for every technological advance, there is a loss. We gain a watch, but lose our knowledge of the stars. We gain an automobile, but lose the use of our legs.

In an age of technological crises, we now need to examine the trade-offs. We need to decide whether the alleged progress liberates or oppresses us. Henry David Thoreau, in the 19th Century, was already worried on this score. He forces us to ask the critical question: Do we ride on the railroad, or does the railroad ride on us? A student educated in both philosophy and technology stands a chance of successfully addressing that question. Such a student also has a "leg up" on discussing the fascinating connections between the humanities and science—connections that reveal new horizons and new possibilities to explore.

12

Noting The Connections

The darkness remains for what seems an eternity.
Then, suddenly a faint light, as if someone has struck a match.

ONE OF THE MOST satisfying virtues that can be taken from college is the ability to perceive the subtle interrelations among various sectors of human knowledge. When that happens, a fascinating coherence and structure begins to emerge within the bewildering maze of ideas that constitute the intellectual side of college life. Suddenly we spot the connection between Wordsworth and the French Revolution, or between an atom's shape and the structure of the universe. For me, the first such discovery was like watching in awe as a sperm whale surfaced slowly and mysteriously from the deep. "Aha!" I shouted. "I see it, I see it. Beautiful!"

In his *Idea of a University*, Cardinal Newman recognized this phenomenon. "All branches of knowledge are connected together," he said, "because the subject matter of knowledge is intimately united in itself." In other words, the interwoven threads of knowledge constitute a magnificent tapestry. The capacity to sort out the threads, to note the connections, does not develop by chance. It happens only if the student's curiosity has been excited by his earlier collegiate experiences, and only if key faculty have encouraged him to think horizontally as a result of their own interdisciplinary outlook.

The more students gain proficiency in "connection spotting," the more they realize, as most adults do, that it is almost impossible to pigeon hole anything, that almost nothing can be stuck into one single category. Rachel Carson's book *Silent Spring* might be a cautionary work on the environment, but it is also a literary classic. Herman Melville's *Moby Dick* might be a great American novel, but a large part of it is also a detailed treatise on the science of whales and the whaling industry. Isaac Asimov's *Fabulous Journey* might be a terrifying account of a miniaturized explorer's adventures, but it is also a physiological analysis of every nook and contour of the human body.

It is similarly difficult to distinguish new ideas from old. Almost all "new" ideas have their roots in the past. The doctrine of "passive resistance" advanced by Martin Luther King in *Letter from a Birmingham Jail* was inspired by Mahatma Ghandi's civil rights campaign in India. Ghandi in turn drew his concepts from Thoreau's *Civil Disobedience* (1846), which declared that governments could be forced to reform if enough people of conscience filled the jails. The roots of such views go back to the 10th Century and St. Augustine, who argued that when human and divine laws conflict, the latter must be given priority. Sophocles had earlier expressed the same view in his drama *Antigone*. There the title character defies human law in the person of King Creon, and buries her brother as dictated by the law of the gods.

There are few more joyful adventures than tracing the evolution of such ideas. The more we gain proficiency in noting the connections, the more we also come to realize how one field of knowledge can illuminate another, even when the two fields are considered wholly disparate. Business, for example, can illuminate literature.

For three years I was a moderator at the Aspen Institute of Humanistic Studies in Colorado. My students were business executives, studying everything from Plato to Arthur Miller's *All My Sons*. On one occasion we were discussing Friedrich Durrenmatt's *The Visit*. It's a German play about Clara, a wicked woman who plans to destroy her hometown because she hates an early lover who still lives there. I remember a businessman turning to me and saying, "You know, that woman is sure one fantastic long-range planner." I was surprised. I had never heard that expression applied to a literary figure. But I got to thinking, there's something to that. Next year when I was back at college teaching Durrenmatt as part of world literature, I said to my class, "You know, the central character in this play is sure one fantastic long-range planner."

Another time at Aspen, we were studying Sophocles' *Antigone,* already referenced above. For me the play is a forerunner of the feminist movement. In the midst of the discussion, one of the businessmen said, "The way I see it, the central character in this play isn't Antigone, it's King Creon." "Why is that?" I asked. The businessman replied, "Because he's a very poor decision maker." "How so?" I said. The man answered, "Well, his emotions are warped by his dislike of women, and he's always surrounded by 'yes-men.'" "What do you mean?" I said. "The group of people that follow him around and keep agreeing with him," he said. "Oh, that's the Greek Chorus," I said. "In Greek tragedy it's a convention to have the Chorus echo the leader." My "student" was now getting agitated. "Well," he insisted, "I don't give a damn if it's a Greek Chorus or not, they're always agreeing with him." "That's very true," I conceded.

So the next fall when I got back to college and was discussing Sophocles as part of world literature, I said to my class, "You know this King Creon is a very poor decision maker. He's always surrounded by yes-men." I learned a great deal about literature from the business executives at Aspen. I came away from these discussions feeling that I had gotten far more than I gave.

When it comes to "noting the connections," colleges were markedly deficient during the first half of this century. In 1958, C. P. (later Lord) Snow, a physicist and novelist, published a seminal work entitled *The Two Cultures,* deploring the gulf between the humanities, especially literature, and the sciences. The joke at the time was that scientists acknowledged Snow as a great writer, while novelists preferred to emphasize his scientific ability. In any event, Snow was largely on target in his charges. During the 1950's literary scholars sneered at engineers' ignorance of Shakespeare, and engineers retorted that humanities people couldn't even change a light bulb.

An episode at the University of Cincinnati illustrates both the problem and the start of a solution. Shortly after I arrived at that institution in 1960, a small group of engineering majors came to me as the new liaison between the liberal arts and engineering colleges. They complained that there was virtually no room for the humanities in their demanding curriculum. Yet as juniors they were weary of the steady diet of quantitative courses, and yearned to learn something of non-technical fields. To fill this void, they boldly proposed an extra-curricular program in great books.

As they saw it, a "non-technical" paperback library could be developed, using the St. John's and University of Chicago checklists of the world's classics. Each student who signed up for this "Humanities Reading Program" would select (for free!) any four books from this library to read on his co-op term, when he was off campus getting "hands-on" experience in industry. When students returned for the next semester, they would discuss the books in humanities professors' homes. After four co-op terms, each student would own sixteen books as the nucleus of his non-technical library, and could select four more works as a bonus for completing the program. When I asked where the funds would come from for this bold and imaginative idea, the engineering students smiled and said, "That will be your part of the project." So I became the chairman of the Humanities Reading Program, and set out to raise the funds.

This proposal was supported by the Engineering dean and some of his faculty, but ridiculed by many humanities scholars. The latter argued that engineering students were already overloaded, and that few would sign up for HRP, as it was now called, even if funding could be found. But lo and behold, the funds were found, two-thirds of the four hundred engineering students signed on, and the engineering faculty belatedly demanded that they get free books too!

Even then it was hard to recruit the needed humanities scholars. They argued that engineering students, shaped by technical subjects, would not be able to handle works of any philosophical magnitude. To convince them otherwise, I recorded a group of "technical" students brilliantly dissecting Eric Fromm's *Psychoanalysis and Religion*, and played it for a few literature professors. At first they smelled a hoax; the students involved must be graduate psychology majors in disguise, they said. But the truth emerged, and a goodly portion of humanities faculty were reluctantly pulled across C.P. Snow's academic divide.

Once humanities professors were involved in the project, they were dumbfounded at the gusto with which engineering students tore into this material. Discussions ranged from Aristotle to Thomas Mann. Inspired by their students, the professors raised such questions as: What have you learned from Aristotle (or whomever) that is relevant to your own field, or to your life as an intelligent learner or good citizen? How are you wiser now about your relationship to yourself, your colleagues, your society, your God? What connections do you see among the books you and your colleagues read during this co-op term?

One liberal arts professor who had volunteered for these home based bull sessions called me at midnight and asked, "How do I get these engineers out of my house? They've eaten all the doughnuts and they're *still* talking!" To everyone's astonishment, the zest of the engineering students transformed the jaded boredom of certain humanities professors into a renewed zest for their own material. As one of them enthusiastically said to me, "Hey, if this stuff can excite engineers, it's got to be good."

There is irony in my experiences with the engineering and business worlds. I had accepted the chairmanship of the Cincinnati HRP program, and I had jumped at the opportunity to moderate great books for businessmen at Aspen, under the illusion that I would be bringing the cultural gospel to the Philistines. In point of fact, it was almost the reverse. Because of their special perspectives, I learned that business and engineering students can bring to literature a Chaucerian gusto, a disconcerting but delightful practicality, and a whole range of fresh and provocative insights. My intermittent contact with business and engineering students over the years not only enriched my own teaching, but more importantly, it radically changed my attitude toward the teaching of students outside the liberal arts.

The gains at the University of Cincinnati notwithstanding, there will always be some two-culture divide, but it will never again be as wide as it was when C.P. Snow spoke out in the 1950's. To highlight the inherent differences, let's compare literature, especially poetry, and biology. Biologists examine nature objectively and impersonally. They analyze and dissect. By contrast, poets examine nature subjectively, emotionally. They are interested not so much in the object itself as in its emotional impact upon them. From the poet's point of view, the scientist often destroys myth, romance, and beauty. Thus Walt Whitman, in "When I Heard the Learned Astronomer," tires of the speaker's technicalities, leaves the lecture hall, goes out into the night, and "looks up at the perfect splendor of the stars."

Biologists, like scientists in general, also speak literally. They use precise terminology. When biologists say "cat," they mean just that, a furry four-footed animal. But poets might mean something else when they use the word. They speak in metaphor, analogy. They see similarities in things normally thought to be dissimilar. Thus, for Carl Sandburg, "the fog comes in on little *cat* feet." Similarly, Amy Lowell describes ripples in a lake as "dragon scales"; John Ciardi once told me that a pine cone was a wooden rose; and for Robert Frost, birch trees, bent low by the snow, looked like "women on their hands and knees, with their hair thrown over their heads to dry in the sun."

Biologists and other scientists are also interested in practical causes and effects. In the 1930's, Urey and the Russians discovered that cells could be reproduced by passing electrical current through certain chemical compounds. When they advanced this discovery as a new theory of creation, a number of critics immediately asked, "Where did the current and chemicals come from?" Urey is reported to have shrugged indifferently and quipped, "Ask the theologians." By contrast, the poet's concerns are the moral and religious implications. In "Mending Wall," Frost's interest is not the wall as such, but the wall as a symbol of the prejudices that separate us from our neighbors. Similarly in *Moby Dick* Melville's interest is not the white whale as such, but as a symbol of demonic forces let loose in the world.

No wonder that the two cultures view each other suspiciously. No wonder there is a chasm of misunderstanding between them. How reconcile the two approaches? How bridge the chasm? We bridge it first of all by noting that the differences have been overstated. Poets and novelists and artists of all types have no monopoly on moral concerns. Biologists have been in the forefront of the environmental movement. The scientists, engineers, managers, and air force personnel who developed, built, and then dropped the nuclear bomb were deeply concerned about the moral implications. Oppenheimer lost his job over the issue, Einstein wrote to Roosevelt, and one member of the air crews wound up in a sanitarium because of his anguish over the human and material destruction at Hiroshima and Nagasaki.

We also bridge the chasm by emphasizing that literary and scientific people have common interests. There are no more observant students of botany and zoology than poets and novelists. Witness Dylan Thomas' herons, and Yeats' "Swans at Coole." Faulkner's most famous short story is "The Bear," and Hemingway's novels feature fish and big game almost as much as people. Elephants, rhinoceroses, and hyenas were not just literary devices for him; he had a kinship with certain animals that most people fear or hate. The great writers have also been fascinated with evolution. "I have a wolf in me," shouts Carl Sandburg in his poem, "Wilderness." Along the same line, William Vaughan Moody describes a drunken tramp who crawls under a circus tent after the show. As he staggers upright before the animal cages, the apes, monkeys, and orangutans begin to laugh hysterically. They cannot believe that this pathetic little man, standing in his dirty, baggy trousers, represents the apex of the evolutionary process.

Literature and science have another thing in common—an appreciation for structure. For the scientists, structure holds the world together. In biology, the basic structural unit is the cell; in physics, the atom; in astronomy, the regular movement of the stars. Likewise, for the writer, structure holds the poem or story together. In poetry, the structure can be anything from rhyme to stanza to free verse. In a story, it can be anything from the author's frame to first person narrative to flashback. Rudyard Kipling used all of these devices in *The Man That Would Be King*. Many critics believe that only through structure does a poem or story have any meaning. Thus John Ciardi's provocative book, *How a Poem Means*.

Most important of all, literature and science share the act and joy of creation. Scientific activity, research, and discovery are in their own ways creative. I know from my own experience. For a year or more I was an applied scientist serving as a navigator of a B-24 in China, flying for seventeen hours in pitch darkness, shooting stars, plotting fixes, and giving headings. Imagine the last half hour of such a flight. A final heading and ETA (estimated time of arrival) are given to the pilot. Then I climb into the nose of the plane, peer out, and see utter darkness. The black remains for what seems an eternity. The tension is acute. Then, suddenly a faint light, as if someone struck a match. It's the airfield beacon! Not straight ahead, of course, but close enough, thank God, to turn in on and land. I have written some poems in my time, but none has produced as much creative joy as bringing that plane back home.

Since the 1960's, when the University of Cincinnati started its "Humanities Reading Program for Engineers," there has been a gathering movement to recognize the interconnections between science and the humanities. Lord Snow, the man who first stated the problem, was among the first to offer a solution. In a speech at Ithaca College in 1970, and in private conversations with a few of us afterwards, he urged the development of a new kind of school, exclusively for musicians and mathematicians. "Their thought structure is the same," he said. "Bring them together and the sparks will fly." To test Snow's views, I brought a variety of UB mathematicians, engineers, and musicians to my home for an evening symposium. The speaker was David Barnett, a noted classical composer. When Barnett concluded his remarks, a spirited discussion ensued which awesomely revealed the commonality of interest in the subject. The sparks did fly all right, especially when the participants got into an argument over the definition of symphonic music. Ginny finally pushed them out the door at 2:00 A.M. in the morning.

The UB symposium was stimulating, but a minor event in the increasing effort to bridge the two cultures by insisting that they represented complementary, not opposing, kinds of knowledge. In 1974, David P. Billington, a civil engineering professor at Princeton, began arguing that engineering was "an important component of liberal education." To prove it, he developed a course entitled, "Structure of Urban Environment," which treated engineering as an art form, combining mechanics, politics, art, and architecture. This course had the highest student rating at Princeton for three consecutive years.

In 1987, the first conference of a Society for Literature and Science was held at Worcester Polytechnic Institute. According to Snow's *Two Cultures*, these two fields are so different that no worthwhile study can be made of one using techniques of the other. At the new Society's first meeting, this most famous of Snow's contentions was addressed and repudiated. One of the first books published by Society members, *Chaos Bound* by Katherine Hayles of the University of Iowa, documented the common interest of science and literature in disorder and how to control it.

In 1990, the powerful American Association for the Advancement of Science published a much discussed report entitled "The Liberal Art of Science." It demanded that science be integrated into the general curriculum, and that it be broadened to encompass the history, philosophy, sociology, politics, and economics of science and technology. Inspired by this report, the University of California at San Diego inaugurated a "Science Studies" major, aimed at the cultural influences shaping scientific theory. A multi-disciplinary team drawn from science, sociology, philosophy, and history teaches the courses. One of the history professors, Martin J.S. Rudwick, describes this program as "an attempt to get a dialogue going between disciplines that, if not at war, were ignoring each other."

As such developments suggest, colleges are far better prepared today than they were fifty years ago to help students "make the connections." Before World War II, higher education institutions were rigidly organized by departments, and interdisciplinary courses were infrequent. Today, some schools, like the University of Wisconsin at Eau Claire, are seeking to blur the distinctions among departments with courses like "Writing to Explore Nursing." Other schools like Stockton State in New Jersey have been founded on the basis of interdisciplinary divisions and majors, with a trend toward interdisciplinary courses which are problem-oriented and taught by multi-disciplinary teams.

Even at institutions which have stuck by the traditional departments, interdisciplinary centers have often evolved in such fields as aging and venture management. In the first instance, UB nurses, biologists, psychologists, sociologists, counselors, and business professors were drawn together to explore such questions as: What are the myths and realities of getting older? How does aging or aging parents affect the performance of employees? What policies should corporations develop in this regard? In the second instance, Wharton School professors of management law, science, engineering, economics, and even the humanities sought to broker partnerships between inventors and venture capitalists, some of whom were once literature or music students!

The establishment of such centers has been a wise move, because modern problems require multi-disciplinary solutions. Protection of the environment, for example, involves historical, socio-economic, political, scientific, legal, and philosophical issues. Solving such a problem involves the perspectives of many academic disciplines, all working in close harmony toward a common end. Another sign that noting connections is now *de rigueur* is the welcome increase in "barrier-busting" examinations—i.e, "horizontal" exams, which compel the student to transcend walls erected by traditional departments. Back in the 1950's, when I first experimented with such exams at Hanover College, the students were enraged, and complained to the administration. The only time they were angrier was when I declared extra "bonus classes" to celebrate the college football team's undefeated season.

Outside the classroom, in their research and writings, mathematicians are now analyzing the logic of humor, while their fellow scientists are moving closer to religion. Physicists are exploring universal laws as evidence of God's existence. Biologists are focusing on the miracle of life as proof of some type of divinity. Zoologists are now conceding that the Book of Genesis, taken allegorically, is an accurate account of evolution. In the wider world beyond the Ivory Tower, churches are merging "ecumenically" as they perceive common doctrines. Socialist states like China, Russia, even Myramar (Burma), are embracing the Western free enterprise system. Formerly sovereign nations, sensing common problems, are moving toward varying degrees of federation in Asia, Europe, Africa, and Latin America. Despite wars, terrorism, and international crises, the modern trend is unmistakably "horizontal" toward interconnections, coming together, closure. Students who have been sensitized to perceive these trends will hold a considerable advantage over fellow graduates who still suffer from the delusion that everything is vertical and separate.

Despite the connections which make learning come alive, there remain crucial differences between the humanistic and scientific approaches. The point is that both are valuable, because each serves a different human need. The humanities appeal to our imaginative and affective side; the sciences to our reason and intellect. What colleges should teach is that no person can be a whole person without both. Those who learn to become "whole persons" will automatically develop open minds, because they will have discovered the "unity of knowledge" that Newman proclaimed.

13

Open Minds

*Franklin once told the story of a man who had
one handsome and one deformed leg.*

A NOTED PROFESSOR of political science once said to me, "You can talk all you want, but you'll never change my mind." He was obviously playing God. Because St. Augustine, in the *City of God,* says that the only immovable object is the deity himself. If we are talking with another intelligent, well-informed person, we must concede the possibility of being persuaded to change our mind. The difference between the scholar (in a broad sense) and the fanatic is that the former's mind is open despite his learning, while the latter's is closed despite his ignorance.

Humility is a pre-requisite for an open mind. If we think we know everything, why listen to anyone else? The educated person's constant question should be: "What do *you* think?" My favorite recollection of humility is Fernec Nagy, one-time premier of Hungary. He was forced out by the Communists, and came to Alfred to speak after taking a post at Harvard in urban planning. Because of campus problems, I had to desert him after his speech. When I returned home late that night, there he was, reading in my library. When I chastised him for not going to bed, he replied, "In my country the guest never goes to bed until his host does." When I asked him why, he smiled and said, "Because the guest has much to learn from his host." "And vice versa," I said with a grin. We talked for awhile, learning from each other. I never saw him again. But I remember his kindness and modesty—qualities not always associated with men of brilliance and courage.

Each year Ginny and I browse among the books at Fairfield's Pequot Library Festival, a gargantuan secondhand book sale. People come from as far as Ohio and Michigan to grab nuggets for fifty cents or a dollar. Every year, we promise "just to look," not to buy. I have already given half my library to Juniata, and the other half is sprawled all over the shelves, desks, tables, chairs, closets and floors of our home. The last thing I need is another book.

So we roam for two hours through the Pequot Library tents, fingering some of the 100,000 or so donated volumes. They are mind-bogglingly classified as religion/philosophy, performing arts, diet/nutrition, crafts/hobbies, Connecticut history, foreign language, travel, mystery, sports, animals, fiction, nature, science, business/engineering, astrology/occult, photography, literature, biology, history, art/architecture, cars/trains/planes, medical/psychology, education, military, classics, cooking, and erotica. The foregoing are just a few of the more important subjects.

I skip over a lot of these sections every year, especially "cooking," because in the era of modern feminism, it might be unwise to learn too much in that field. "Classics" always lures me, of course. It's like saying hello to old friends. "Erotica" was added just this year. A number of older folk, just out from church, were timidly scanning certain thin but torrid volumes. I was tempted but skipped "Erotica," fearing that someone might snap a photo of me deeply engrossed in Henry Miller or Anais Nin.

Despite our promise to "just look," I wound up buying *The Undergraduate Experience in America* (understandable, given the subject of this book), *The Shroud of Turin* (understandable, given my ten-year debate with scientists over the allegedly Christ-related linen cloth), and Kahil Gilbran's *The Prophet* (*not* understandable, given that I already have several volumes of this work, but Ginny was touched by the mother to daughter letter written on the flyleaf, so what could I do?) Ginny was equally extravagant, buying the *Word and Expression Locator* (she always wonders if she's using the right word), *Discoveries in Archaeology* (she's especially interested in King Tut), and *All-Time Salad Recipes* (she makes a mean salad, and wants to maintain her reputation). The whole lot, counting three hot dogs and two lemonades, was $17.50.

Why am I telling you all this? Because each year, having spent two hours among these 100,000 volumes (plus fifteen minutes for the hot dogs), I come away realizing how incredibly ignorant I am. Oh sure, I recognize a title or two here and there, but if I were to read ten of those books every day for the next twenty years, the result would be less than a drop in the ocean of expanding knowledge. Today even the most learned person knows an infinitesimally small piece of the whole. Each of us clings to a narrow spar in the midst of the ocean. Per my earlier comment to Captain Boyle of the *Metapan* (Chapter 1), Socrates was wise beyond words when he said, "A wise man knows that he knows not."

Socrates was willing to learn from anybody, and we should do likewise. "Listen to others, even the dull and ignorant; they too have their story," reads an inscription in St. Paul's Church in Baltimore. When I first started teaching T.S. Eliot's *The Wasteland*, I was stumped by the line, "The river's tent is broken." I had no idea what it meant, and unfortunately, there was no teacher's guide to make me look brilliant in front of my students. After I ventured a foolish interpretation in class, a young woman, who was anything but "dull and ignorant," raised her hand and said respectfully, "Sir, I thought it meant that it was fall and all the leaves had blown off the trees bordering the Thames." My heart leaped. My God, the girl was right! The next year, when we came to that passage, I said to the class matter-of-factly, "Obviously, Eliot means here that it is fall and all the leaves, etc. . . ."

Another of the marks of a truly educated person is his willingness to gather evidence, and to let that evidence guide his conclusion. In coming to any conclusion, especially on a major issue, it's especially important to listen to those who hold contrary views. Even if the other person is wrong, his wrongness will better help us understand the rightness of our own position. And if he's right, and we don't listen to him, we've lost the opportunity to exchange our error for his truth. More frequently we'll each have a piece of the truth. By sharing our views, we can each profit from what the other knows. These aren't my ideas. They come from an essay by the philosopher John Stuart Mill. The title: "On Liberty of Thought." It's a classic, and everybody should read it.

What Mill is really saying is that nobody is always wrong. I was once on a tour bus in London. The guide pointed off to the left as we passed slowly by and said, "That's the famous Brontë home." "Emily Brontë?" a little old lady sitting opposite me asked brightly. "No," said the driver. "*Charlotte* Brontë. When she came to London to seek a publisher." "Oh," said the lady, a trace of disappointment in her voice at being wrong. The bus continued on for a mile or so and the guide pointed toward the right. "Now there's the well know Johnson house," he said. The old lady paused a second, screwed up her courage, and asked, "Ben Jonson?" "No," said the guide with some annoyance. "*Samuel* Johnson. When Boswell was doing the famous biography of him." "Oh," whispered the lady, embarrassed now to have been mistaken a second time. Finally, a few miles farther on, the guide pointed through the expansive windshield and exclaimed proudly, "And that, ladies and gentlemen, is Christ Church, one of the finest examples of late Gothic architecture in England." The little lady hesitated in anguish. Her spark of inquisitiveness had almost been extinguished. At that crucial moment an American soldier sitting in the seat behind tapped her on the shoulder and said, "Go ahead, lady. Try once more. You can't be wrong all the time!"

An open mind seeks to strike a balance in addressing any matter. College should help students to develop a balanced view by exposing them to the many sides of a given issue; by insisting that they patiently probe, dig beneath the surface, and avoid snap judgments; and by stressing that there are many kinds of excellence, all of them admirable. Kentucky State College, an incubator of regional leaders, is just as excellent in its way as Harvard is in its. KSC provides a service that Harvard could not and would not provide. Unfortunately, the snob believes in only one standard of excellence—his own. He is a variation of the fanatic. Both have closed minds and therefore a distorted view of life.

The aim of education, as Matthew Arnold noted, is to help us "see life steadily, and see it *whole.*" "Whole" means to address all the viewpoints on a given problem, not just the viewpoint we happened to grow up with. Most of us were brought up to venerate Columbus. But Honduran Indians detest him, as the forerunner of five centuries of genocide. Given such disagreements, "on the other hand" is a frequent comment among people who seek a fair balance in their thinking. Economists and professors are especially fond of this expression. President Eisenhower once said he yearned to meet a one-handed economist, who could give him straight answers. I once met the wife of Norman Eliason, my Old English instructor at the University of North Carolina.

"It must be fun to live with such a brilliant man," I said. "Well, it's more frustrating than fun," she replied. "Norman makes everything so complicated. You ask him if he wants a ham sandwich for lunch, and he says, well, on the one hand, yes, but. . . ." One of the most memorable examples of balance in literature is this thrilling passage from Thomas Wolfe's *You Can't Go Home Again*:

> Here, then, is man, this moth of time, this dupe of brevity and numbered hours, this travesty of waste and sterile breath. Yet if the gods could come here to a desolate, deserted earth where only the ruin of man's cities remained, where only a few marks and carvings of his hand were legible, a cry would burst out of their hearts and they would say: "He lived, and he was here!"

An open mind not only seeks to strike a balance, it is also willing to change its view if circumstances change, or new information becomes available. The aim of the open mind is to steer between fickleness on the one hand (oops!) and wrong-headed stubbornness on the other. On many occasions, I have been wrong in my perceptions, and was fortunately embarrassed into changing them. In one instance, I was attending a formal dinner in London, and complained to all who would listen that the Queen never smiled during the Trooping the Colors ceremony. My tablemate, a buxom English matron, was visibly upset. "Have you ever seen a military review?" she asked sharply. "Well, yes." I replied. "At such an event," she persisted, "does the general ever smile at his troops?" "Well, no." I said feebly, realizing that I was on a limb about to be sawed off.

I still think the Queen should smile more on public occasions, but concede now that Trooping the Colors should be an exception. Imagine hundreds of guardsmen astride magnificent black horses, sweeping ten abreast in a tight, fast-paced formation before the Queen, plumes jostling, armor and bridles jingling, scarlet tunics and silver helmets gleaming in the sun. On the one occasion when Ginny and I saw this spectacle, one of the nearest horses splattered mud on our nine-year-old Greg's trousers, as he stood just behind a guardrail. Awed by this modest connection to royalty, he refused for weeks to let his pants be washed, preferring instead to point out the mud to his classmates or anyone else who would look or listen.

A second memorable instance when I changed my mind involved my producing and moderating "Casing the Classics" over WHAS-TV in Louisville. My show on great books did not attract commercial sponsors, and was therefore labeled a "public service" program. But the show just before mine had advertisers lined up around the block. Called "T-Bar-V Ranch" and featuring a covered wagon set, it consisted of two "cowboys" (actually University of Louisville graduates) who daily played banjos and sang "Happy Birthday" to children. Indignant that cowboys could get sponsors, while Wordsworth, Dante, and Ibsen could not, I complained to Sam Gifford, WHAS program director. He set me straight with one brief statement. "Lee," he said, "that show makes all the money you lose." This revelation rudely changed my perception. I began to see my rivals in an entirely different light. Without "T-Bar-V Ranch," there would be no "Casing the Classics"! So I got to know the cowboys, told them they were great, and was even invited to sing "Happy Birthday" with them several times.

If there is one word which best describes the open mind, it is "tolerant." The big question is, can a person who is tolerant still hold convictions? Absolutely. A person can be a Christian and still have the greatest respect for Islam and Judaism. One can have tolerance for multiple views and still retain the courage to take a stand on deeply felt principles. The difference between the tolerant and intolerant person is not that the former lacks convictions and the latter has them. The difference is that the tolerant person, being human, recognizes that he might be dissuaded from his opinions through further experience, reading, or human discourse. The intolerant person, with his arrogance or presumed pipeline to the deity, assumes that his thoughts are set in concrete.

A tolerant man or woman recognizes that every idea or belief has some degree of value, even if in a negative sense. John Milton said that we could only tell good because it contrasts with evil. A scale of values is therefore an important component of an open mind. Such a scale is nothing more than a hierarchy of moral choices. Every time we make a decision of any consequence, we are choosing among two or more priorities. This "problem of choice" is magnified when we deal with public policy issues, especially if they involve large sums of money.

For example, the $840 million cost of a Stealth bomber would provide pre-natal care for 950,000 mothers. The $100 million annual operating cost of one aircraft carrier would clean up 28 major toxic waste sites. The $1 billion cost for two attack submarines could provide college grants to 500,000 low-income students. The $200 million that buys four nuclear weapons tests could be used instead to inoculate all of the world's 140 million children born in one year against the six fatal childhood diseases.

Those who choose the military option in each of these instances put "national security" near the top of their values scale. Those who choose the alternate uses of the available funds give humanitarian needs a higher priority. No matter which alternative is chosen, there is always a trade off, that is, something which is valuable but considered less worthy is rejected, and sometimes lost forever. According to Dostoevsky in *Crime and Punishment*, most of us would put our own life at the top of our scale of values, and therefore are willing to sacrifice any principle to stay alive. Not so Lord Chancellor Thomas More, who saw his belief in the Pope's headship of the 16th Century English Church as more important than his own life. He therefore cheerfully accepted his execution, rather than recant.

Ginny and I learned of a similar situation when we visited the Alcazar in Toledo, Spain, some years ago. This formidable structure had been a government fort during the Spanish Civil War in the 1930's. Despite brutal bombardment and the deaths of many of the garrison, the fort commander, a colonel, was ordered not to surrender. In desperation the enemy forces captured the colonel's son, and the following phone conversation then ensued (visitors can hear a tape of the actual conversation in the original Spanish or in a translation): *Enemy Officer:* "Colonel, we have your son. Surrender the fort or we will kill him." *Fort Commander:* "Put my son on the line." *Son:* "I'm here, Papa, and afraid." *Fort Commander:* "Son, be brave, and prepare to die."

Many of us would no doubt react differently in a similar situation. But that's the point. Everybody's scale of values is different and highly personalized, based on parental upbringing, temperament, church and political allegiances, and education or the lack of it. If you asked ten people from various vocations and backgrounds to prioritize the importance to them of money, fame, high office, career, life, integrity, sex, love, marriage, children, community service, and the like, every person would arrange these values in a different order. What some see as valuable, others see as worthless. In Thomas More's *Utopia*, gold is relegated to children's toys and trinkets.

Not long ago, I gave a talk to a class of Eagle Scouts. Afterwards, George Oldroyd, then a stout fifteen-year-old youngster with merit badges running all the way round to his fanny, came up and thanked me for my comments. He groped in his trouser pockets and pulled out a two-inch piece of dirty tallow candle. He explained that it had been used in his Order of the Arrow initiation. "This is the only thing of value I have," he said soberly. "Please take it." What a dilemma! For two months I kept that dirty piece of candle on my desk. Twice I rescued it from the trash after the cleaning lady dumped it. To the young Scout, the piece of candle was as valuable as the gold, incense, and myrrh brought by the Wise Men to the Christ Child. How could I throw it away?

Some people, like George Oldroyd, exalt lowly things, thereby making them important. Others do the reverse. On my suggestion, Theodore Roosevelt McKeldin, then Governor of Maryland and my old Sunday School teacher, was once invited to Hanover College to give a speech on George Washington, and to receive an honorary degree. To warm up the audience, the Governor began the speech with an Irish joke. The audience was so delighted that he decided to forget Washington and speak on Ireland instead. In an hour discourse on the latter subject, he told a series of increasingly off-color Irish stories. The audience responded with hysterical laughter. On stage, however, the college president (then Albert Parker) and the faculty sat in stunned silence, some of them glaring at me as the perpetuator of this inappropriate comedy.

Having made a big impression (to put it mildly) with his speech, McKeldin then ambled over to President Parker's house, and regaled the guests by showing them his second suitcase, which contained several honorary degree hoods picked up from other colleges on his way to Hanover. Lifting the lid, he tossed in the multi-colored Hanover hood, explaining that he was going to "have the whole bunch made into a bed quilt." Dr. Parker never again asked me to suggest honorary degree candidates.

In the last analysis, it is of course impossible to have a wholly open mind, a completely balanced view. If we must err, which way should we tilt? I was once in a Midwestern town for a lecture engagement, and asked two people, "How are folks in this town?" The first person, a short-order cook, snarled, "Rotten." The second person, a hotel clerk, smiled and said, "Pretty nice, by and large." As Emily Dickinson might have said, one person had manure in his soul and the other, rose petals. If I had to choose between the two, I'd choose the rose petals every time.

So would Ben Franklin. In the 18th Century, men's trousers came down to just below the knee, so the calf was on display. At the time, women often spoke of a man's "nice turn of leg." Against this backdrop, Franklin once told the story of a man who had one handsome and one deformed leg. He would hold large parties, and sit prominently in the hall as his guests entered. If they commented on his deformed leg, the host wrote their names in a black book, reserved for those who could see only the ugliness in life. If they commented on the handsome leg (for example, "Hey fellow, you've got a whopper of a limb there" or however they said it in those days), the host wrote their names in a white book, reserved for those who saw only beauty in human existence. Only the latter ever got invited back.

Of course, guests with a truly balanced view would have seen *both* legs—the handsome and the deformed. Those are the ones whom I would have invited to *my* party, had I been the host. But as Franklin knew, Americans lean too far on the debunking side; they need more of Wordsworth's sense of wonder. All of us need to be more like the little girl to whom the whole countryside seemed full of miracles—especially the sight (as she later reported to her mother) of ten little pigs blowing up a big pig. A model for all of us is another little girl who got lost in Macy's. The frantic mother finally found her walking hand in hand with a couple of traditionally dressed nuns. "I hope she hasn't bothered you," said the embarrassed mother. "Oh no," said one of the nuns, smiling. "You see, she thinks we're a pair of penguins."

Among the gifts that a college should give its graduates are an open mind, a balanced view, and a sense of wonder. As Georgia O'Keeffe taught us, it is not anti-intellectual to see beauty *amidst* the bleakness. In fact, that's what "balance" means. In her paintings of the barren New Mexico desert, she helps all of us to appreciate the wondrous mystery and formidable strength of stark boulders, bleached bones, and treeless hills. But this open mind, this balance and wonder, must be applied not only to our own country, but also to the problems of our planet, beginning with the environment we all share.

14

Spaceship Earth

Hanging from the champion tree-sitter's platform was a massive sign admonishing loggers to "Respect Your Elders."

ARTH HAS ALWAYS been a puny planet, but never so much as now. In the years following World War II we have witnessed exploding population, forced migrations of refugees, increasing competition for limited resources, evolution of multinational corporations, intermeshing of national economics, emergence of regional political systems, and the launching of communication satellites. Even more significantly, we have watched with alarm the development of nuclear leviathans on both sides of the former superpower divide—earth-straddling monsters that far exceed in destructive power the "Little Boy" dropped on Hiroshima on August 6, 1945. To be sure, the U.S. and Russia are now in the process of reducing this fearsome armament. But 500 tons of poorly guarded plutonium remain on the Russian side. What happens if a terrorist group or rogue state obtains some of it?

Clearly the planet is smaller than before. So much so, that C.P. Snow has spoken of "Spaceship Earth," in which all of us are part of the crew, and share the same fragile life support system. Now more than ever, the poet John Donne is right. "No man is an island unto himself. Every man is a piece of the continent. Ask not for whom the bell tolls. It tolls

113

for thee." Updated, that means if anyone is in trouble in Haiti or Afghanistan or South Africa, then we are all in trouble, because we are all interlocked with one another in an unprecedented way.

As we read Donne, we suddenly realize that there are few significant national problems left. Almost everything is international in scope. The problems of food, population, poverty, energy, raw materials, space, trade, pollution, drugs, and disease—all of these transcend nations and can only be resolved by international cooperation. This new interdependence especially applies to the environment. The Mediterranean fruit fly is no respecter of national borders. Neither are the radioactive clouds from the disaster at Chernobyl.

Earth is not only smaller than it used to be. It is also more vulnerable. It is at risk from many directions, but the chief enemy is its own inhabitants. In 1992, 1500 scientists, including more than half of the living Nobel laureates, warned that "human beings and the natural world are on a collision course." The truth of this "Warning to Humanity" lies all around us. For starters, our reckless burning of coal, oil, and other fossil fuels is trapping heat in the atmosphere. The result is increasing temperatures, which over time could induce polar melting, and cause everything from drought in Iowa to floods in Florida.

Scientists are split on the extent to which humans are responsible for this global warming or "greenhouse effect." But there is broad scientific consensus on ozone depletion, caused by the production of various man-made chemicals that are used in aerosol sprays, refrigerators, and air conditioners. At its most recent seasonal peak, this hole in the ozone layer had grown to eight million square miles—more than twice the size of Canada. According to the UN World Meteorological Organization, it is expanding at a rapid rate, in the process exposing us to increasingly damaging ultraviolet rays. At best this increased exposure means more urban smog and human medical problems, especially asthma, skin cancer, and cataracts. At worst, it means the death of many life forms, including humans.

Not only have we earth-dwellers damaged the heavens; we have also endangered land and water. For years we have cut down the redwoods, strip-mined the hillsides, spilled oil from tankers, sprayed pesticides everywhere, filled rivers with effluent, and turned lakes into scum. Our over-pumping of ground water has caused shortages (and conflicts) in 80 countries comprising two-fifths of the world's population. Outmoded agricultural practices have degraded 40 percent of the world's vegetative surface—an area larger than India, China, and the former Soviet Union combined. In Brazil and elsewhere, we have burned and slashed tropical rain forests so rapidly that if we continue, most will be gone by the end of the next century, along with a large number of plant and animal species. Human activities are now driving species extinction at the rate of *several per hour*—thousands of times faster than evolution can create new species. In fact, by 2100, the earth could suffer the irreversible loss of one third of all species now living.

Such threats have driven some Earth Firsters to unusual behavior. Julia Hill, for example, lived through the winter of 1998 on a small platform, perched in an ancient redwood 180 feet above a paint slash marking the tree for logging. Hanging from the champion tree-sitter's platform was a massive sign admonishing loggers to "Respect Your Elders." According to the 3/29/98 *New York Times,* Julia was armed with electric socks to ward off the cold, a cell phone to conduct radio interviews, and a propane stove to cook Mexican dinners. The *Times* compared her to the "lady conservationists" of 1925, who "first enraged loggers by chaining themselves to trees."

To such behavior, cynics often reply, "So what? Who, other than a few extremists, cares about redwoods—or the spotted owl?" Such comments reflect ignorance of the extensive life support services that humanity derives from nature. From our ecosystems, including the spotted owl, we obtain food, timber, and fibers. As Paul Ehrlich has noted, nature underpins agricultural productivity, provides most of our pharmaceuticals, purifies air and water, mitigates against drought and floods, generates and preserves soils, decomposes waste, pollinates crops, and controls pests. (See *Atlantic Monthly,* December 1997.) These crucial services operate in such subtle and intricate ways that most could not be replaced by technology. In addition to these practical contributions, the world's biological systems make possible the astonishing beauty of the earth so many of us delight in.

When I was a boy, I spent the summers with a sea captain grandfather on Tilghman's Island on the Eastern Shore of Maryland. "Cap'n," as my mother called him, gave me a rowboat, which was more majestic to me in those days than an ocean liner was later. Every morning I would pack a lunch and row away into the mist of the Chesapeake Bay's coves, bays, and estuaries, looking for mussels, clams, and especially soft shell crabs to bring back to my grandfather. One of my most vivid memories is of Cap'n eating a crab sandwich, the legs and fins sticking out from the bread. Ugh, I thought then. A delicacy, I know now. From my rowboat, I saw hardhead, rock, and bluefish; swamps, marshes, scrub pines, and beach plum brush; snowy egrets wading patiently for their breakfasts; and great blue herons lumbering awkwardly into the sky like ancient creatures from some distant past. Even with the Bay Bridge across the Chesapeake, much of the Shore's idyllic character remains. But for how long, given the polluting run-off from shoreline chicken farms and the over-harvesting of oysters?

Simultaneous with the civilian havoc we have wreaked over the earth, thousands of earth dwellers have waged 170 regional wars since World War II, killing 45 million people (mostly innocent civilians), destroying huge tracts of land, contaminating water and pockmarking arable farmland with millions of anti-personnel mines, whose chief victims have been women and children. Meanwhile, the two superpowers (one current, one former), while avoiding nuclear holocaust, have become the chief military polluters of the earth.

Through our manufacture and testing of weapons, millions of tons of toxic waste have destroyed thousands of square miles in both Russia and the U.S., turning many areas into quarantined "sacrifice zones." In 1958, a Russian nuclear installation exploded in the Ural Mountains, devastating the countryside for hundreds of miles. The area immediately became a radioactive wasteland. It was fenced off, and nobody can live there for thousands of years. In 1959, the U.S. Department of Agriculture announced that U.S. and Soviet atom tests had scattered radioactive plutonium (the basic fuel for nuclear bombs) over the entire earth. The Department noted that these radioactive particles were now in the bodies of all human beings, regardless of age and country. In 1962, The *Bulletin of Atomic Scientists* revealed that children then growing up in the United States had at least eight times more plutonium radioactivity in their bones than children in prior generations. The scientists concluded that if this trend continued, the mutation of genes might be so great that future humans would not resemble current members of the race.

The signs of potential trouble are all around if we care to look. Consider these chronological scenes: It is 1954. John Wayne and a company of actors make a motion picture in Utah, near an atomic testing area.

They and the production crew breathe dust from plutonium bomb tests. A quarter of a century later, John Wayne is dead of cancer, as are most of the Utah company. The number dead is far beyond statistical probability. 1970. A small town doctor in Colorado discovers that every child he is treating has some sort of birth defect. He can't figure it out. Then he discovers what is wrong. The homes of these children have been built on waste rock from a mining field for uranium, the "trigger" in nuclear bombs. 1981. A famous woman physician writes that if present trends continue, the air we breathe, the food we eat, the water we drink will soon be contaminated with enough radioactive fallout to pose a health hazard far greater than any plague that humanity has ever experienced.

Such evidence suggests that we are slowly killing the human race, even without a nuclear exchange. According to the Center for Defense Information, staffed by retired admirals and generals, the U.S. and Russia have not only risked our health by the manufacture and testing of weapons, but also by their accident-prone deployment. "Fail-safe" is a macabre joke which exists only in the military manuals. Aircraft loaded with nuclear weapons have rolled off carriers and disappeared into the sea. Nuclear submarines have leaked reactor coolant and sunk to the ocean floor. Twenty-four-megaton bombs (equal to seventy Nagasakis) have fallen from B-52's into North Carolina and Georgia swamps. In one case, the weapon was recovered; five of the six safety mechanisms had broken on impact. In another, the bomb could not be located. So the Air Force built a fence around the swamp, and designated it a "nuclear safety zone." George Orwell, in *1984*, could not have imagined a better piece of "double-speak."

Sadly, many of the 170 wars since World War II, especially those in Lebanon, the Middle East, and Bosnia, have been fought in the name of religion—Christianity, Islam, and Judaism. The Christian churches in particular have been largely mute on peace and chiefly negative on environment. Most Episcopalians are unaware that their own Prayer book contains this entreaty: "God, give us all a reverence for the earth as your creation, that we may use its resources rightly in the service of others and to your honor and glory." Prayer Books notwithstanding, the Christian faith has over the centuries fostered a careless attitude toward the earth. Christianity's focus on heaven and the afterlife undercuts the importance of the world we inhabit while alive. Not until the 1980's and '90's did theologians make a major effort to right the balance. In 1994, for example, Sallie McFague of Vanderbilt University set the theological world on its ear with a book partly entitled, *An Ecological Theology*, which described earth metaphorically as "the body of God."

It is amazing how similar Professor McFague's views are to those of Chief Seattle of the Squamish Indians, who more than a century earlier, in 1851, gave the following response (shortened and slightly rearranged) to a proposed land-purchase treaty:

> Every part of this earth is sacred to my people. We are part of the earth and it is part of us. The perfumed flowers are our sisters; the deer, the horse, the great eagle, these are our brothers. We know that the white man does not understand our ways. One portion of land is the same to him as the next. He treats his mother, the earth, and his brother, the sky, as things to be bought, plundered, sold like sheep or bright beads. His appetite will devour the earth and leave behind only a desert. Whatever befalls the earth befalls the sons of the earth. If men spit upon the ground, they spit upon themselves. If you contaminate your bed, you will one night suffocate in your own waste. The earth does not belong to man; man belongs to the earth. This earth is precious to God, and to harm the earth is to heap contempt on its Creator.

For decades, as we abused the earth, it always snapped back. But now the global food supply is dwindling. The three primary food-producing sectors—farms, livestock, and fisheries—are declining. Beef production, potable water, and fish catches have dropped significantly since the 1980's. The abuse has begun to boomerang. As Chief Seattle predicted, we have fouled our own nest, and we must now confront the inevitable result: mother earth is losing her resiliency. Pogo got it right in the old comic strip: "We have met the enemy, and they is us."

Can the enemy's technology now save the day? It is unlikely. Natural resources are finite. Global warming aside, technology can find remaining coal, and can rapidly extract and distribute it to consumers. *But it cannot create new coal deposits.* Once a natural resource is depleted, it is gone for good. Even with food, technology has its limits.

The per capita production of grain foods, which comprise the bulk of human diet, has declined since 1984—despite the continued conversion of forest land to crop production, and the technology-driven Green Revolution of high yield grains. In fact, the population explosion is largely a result of technological innovations in agriculture and medicine, combined with the humanitarian distribution of food and medical services worldwide.

As just implied, the chief environmental problem is not only the behavior of the earth's inhabitants, but the fact that there are so many of us. The earth's ability to absorb destructive wastes is limited, just as its ability to provide natural resources is finite. Yet population growth is accelerating at a phenomenal rate. In 1960 there were "only" three billion people on earth. In 2000 A.D., according to the U.S. Census Bureau, there are now six billion. Consider that it took many thousands of years for the population to grow to three billion, but it has now taken only forty years to double that growth! Ninety million more people join the human family each year. The World Bank and the United Nations have estimated that population, because of falling fertility rates, will eventually stabilize at twelve to fourteen billion, more than double the almost six billion of today. Yet even now, one person in five lives in absolute poverty, without enough to eat.

Joel Cohen, head of the Population Laboratory at Rockefeller University, raises the key question in the title of his new book, *How Many People Can the Earth Support?* His answer: Not many more, unless we want to irreversibly degrade the environment, or increase the already terrible poverty in much of the habitable world. "Isn't there always a little more space?" people ask. Well sure, if you want eventually to stand in place, sleep on top of each other, and be buried standing up.

The state of the earth is not a laughing matter. But the failure to achieve a zero-growth population has led to a number of comic suggestions, my favorite being that espoused by Donald Allen in *The Reporter* for 1965. Instead of breeding toy poodles, he suggests we breed mini-men and women. If each of us were only eighteen inches tall, he argues, it would solve all the problems of the population explosion. Downsizing humans would greatly reduce food consumption. Full employment would also be achieved, because all of the now oversized houses, cars, roads, and so forth would need to be demolished and rebuilt to the new Lilliputian scale.

The environmental problems described here apply to all countries, but especially to those in the Third World. In the "North" or industrial democracies, belated but admirable steps are now being taken to assure clean air and pure water, reduce smokestack pollution and auto emissions, purify the rivers (including the mighty Hudson!), expand wildlife preserves, protect endangered species, limit the size of families, eliminate nuclear testing, clean up toxic wastes, and move toward the reduction of armament. However, in the "South" or developing countries, few of these things are happening.

In fact, a number of developing states, notably India and Pakistan, are developing their own nuclear potential, and some are even racing to gain an advantage over their neighbors in chemical and biological weapons. Moreover, at the recent Kyoto Conference on Global Warming (December 1997), Third World countries rejected the North's proposal that they reduce the burning of coal and other fossil fuels. Look, they said. You damaged the environment on your way to becoming economic powers. Now you want the poor nations to back off and remain backward. No way! The UN panel on climate change estimates that by 2025, the Third World (absent controls) could be emitting four times the greenhouse gases produced by industrial countries today.

For this and many other reasons, the next century might well decide the future of the earth as a habitation for humans. It is therefore imperative that every college student, regardless of major, be required to take a course on the environment. Such a course should be team taught by a broad array of faculty from the humanities, social studies, and natural sciences, and from engineering, business, diplomacy, ROTC, and law. It should expose in depth the planetary dangers that have been briefly described here. It should also identify and debate current and possible future solutions, so that college graduates can lobby as citizens and future leaders for a safer, cleaner earth for their children and grandchildren in the 21st Century.

Among proposed solutions are moving toward more benign energy sources; expanding conservation and recycling; reducing consumption and food waste; diverting to environmental improvement the one trillion annually spent worldwide on war; stabilizing population by expanding family planning; ensuring that women control their own reproductive decisions; and reducing Third World poverty, which, if not ameliorated, will provoke massive civil unrest, and threaten the security of the developed world. As Paul Ehrlich has noted, "Perpetuating Third World poverty is a luxury that the prosperous can no longer afford."

The debates among faculty and students should focus on how such steps and others could be more rapidly implemented and enforced. Indonesia provides for us a glimpse of an undesirable future. Each year in that country, agricultural developers set fires to the jungle as a cheap way of clearing land for grazing or farming. In recent years these fires have gotten more out of control. In 1997 their smoke merged with urban smog to create a hideous choking haze which enveloped *most of Southeast Asia*, stinging nostrils, burning eyes, and making it difficult to see the nearest person or building even in daytime.

If this type of behavior continues, we will need to take Isaac Asimov's suggestion that we flee to the moon or Mars, where we might be able to survive in underground caves, hanging upside down like bats. Rich or poor, East or West—we are all in the same lifeboat now, and it's leaking. Let's start bailing together, before we sink or the boat overturns. C.P. Snow would of course prefer a different metaphor. He would urge that we fix the life support system before Spaceship Earth implodes.

15

Global Perspective

The spider was 15 feet high, with hairy legs and bulging eyes.

ANY STUDENT WHO hopes to be educated today must learn to think globally—first about the environment, and then about the socio-economic and political state of the world. The starting point for the latter is an understanding of the contrast between "North" and "South." The North, or industrial states, have most of the world's wealth, health, food, toilets, longevity, education, contraceptives, and scientific know-how. The South, or developing nations, have most of the world's population, illiteracy, poverty, hunger, disease, unsanitary conditions, and early mortality. In the Third World, between 30,000 and 40,000 children die *daily* as a result of malnutrition. This miserable situation is exacerbated by the extreme debt of the Southern nations—$100 billion according to reliable sources. To make matters worse, per capita income in the North is ten times that of the South, and the gap is widening. According to the UN, the income ratio of the richest 20 percent of humanity to the poorest 20 percent was 30:1 in 1960. By 1994, the ratio was 80:1.

The United Nations 1996 *Human Development Report* puts the matter bluntly. "An emerging global elite . . . is amassing great wealth and power, while more than half of humanity is being left out. We still have more than half the people on the planet with incomes of less than two dollars a day. For poor people, this two-class world is a breeding ground for hopelessness, anger, and frustration." Consider that only one-fifth of the earth's people live in the North, which is rapidly becoming a velvet-padded ghetto. The world's over-consumption champion is the United States, as reflected in our girths. Americans are 5 percent of the population, but devour 25 percent of the earth's resources. As long as such disparities exist, and especially if they widen, there will be violence, terrorism, revolution, and war. Many of the people living on earth have little to lose from violence. Desperately afflicted by hunger, poverty, and disease, their daily life is already a living hell.

According to an ancient fable, which I first heard at Scout camp, there was once an explorer who went to hell. He found it was a banqueting hall. Emaciated people sat at tables, even though marvelous food was set before them. The explorer noticed with horror what was wrong. Nobody had any arms. Instead, attached to each right shoulder was a wooden spoon. But the people couldn't feed themselves, because when they tried to get the spoon to their mouths, it was too long. So they sat in sullen silence, plotted mischief, and starved. Our explorer then went to heaven and found it was almost exactly the same. Everybody was sitting at tables, nobody had any arms, and everybody had a wooden spoon in place of his right arm. But to the explorer's surprise, the guests were chatting happily, were well-fed, and seemed to be enjoying themselves. Then he discovered what was going on. Each person at the tables, having ladled up some food with his long wooden spoon, was turning and feeding the person next to him, all around the table, each person helping the other.

The point is obvious. If we want a less violent world, with more security for ourselves, then each of us (if only for selfish reasons) must be our brother's keeper. Otherwise we will all sink together into misery, because North and South are interlocked on an ever-shrinking globe where not even a superpower can fend off Third World violence forever. For "Northerners" to be persuaded of this view, they must first possess a global perspective, an intercultural awareness, and a sense of the interdependence of nations and peoples everywhere. These attitudes urgently need to be developed throughout all levels of education, especially through the internationalizing of the college curriculum.

Unfortunately, and with some notable exceptions, colleges have not adjusted swiftly to this global challenge. In 1980, the Educational Testing Service made a study of college seniors, and discovered that 40 percent thought most of the newest nations were located in Europe. Eighty-five percent had little or no knowledge of the oil crisis, world religions, the Bolshevik revolution, developing countries, or human rights violations. Ninety-three percent were not fluent enough in another language to understand a foreign person, even when he was speaking slowly.

Shortly after the ETS study was published, we learned the reason for this international illiteracy. The Council on Learning discovered that only 200 institutions out of 3200 had even the rudiments of an international education. Consequently, less than 5 percent of the U.S. college age group was enrolled in courses which specifically featured international issues. This lack of interest was reflected at the 1983 American Council on Education meeting in Minneapolis, when a few of us sponsored a session on a theme something like, "Should the Universities Confront Global Realities?" Less than twenty presidents attended this session. Everybody else flooded into the room next door, where the subject of federal financial aid was deemed more important than global survival.

During the last decade, the educational landscape has changed. College presidents have gradually recognized that any quality education must simultaneously be international in nature. In the 1990's, it became increasingly obvious that college students would pursue most of their courses in the 21st Century. Why then do we keep giving them a 20th Century education? Admittedly, most colleges today admit foreign students, have international relations clubs, and hold annual UN Days. Many also provide courses on Asia, Latin America, and Africa, and some even consolidate such courses into an Area Study major, so that interested students can explore in depth a single developing region. A few have even started innovative Statesman-in-Residence programs, through which foreign ministers, ambassadors, and sometimes even heads of state visit campuses to discuss their countries' problems and aspirations.

All of these activities are admirable. They provide the needed atmosphere, and most college faculty and administrators rightly encourage them. But at best these efforts affect a small portion of the student body. What is needed, in addition to these peripheral activities, is a wholesale internationalizing of the "general education" courses—i.e., the liberal arts core—required for graduation. Only in this way can we provide an opportunity for *every* student to recognize the importance of a global perspective, not only for his chosen career but also for his life as a citizen and a neighbor.

With apologies to Dartmouth President John Kemeny, who first told this kind of story, let me tell you about a dream I had when I was president of the University of Bridgeport. In the dream, the Archangel Michael came to me. He had in tow an eighteen-year-old girl. He said, "Doctor, this young woman is going to be President of the United States. We are looking for a college that would prepare her for that awesome task. If we entered her at UB, what type of education would you give her, so that she could become an informed and humane world leader?" I was stumped. Nobody, particularly an archangel, had ever asked me that question. I didn't know what to say. Michael looked at me in disgust, and he and the girl disappeared from my dream. As you can imagine, I was mortified. When I woke up, I began to think what a fantastic question! What would a university do if it knew it had a future President of the United States as a student? Especially if it was the first woman president? Obviously she would want to major in political science, or maybe pre-law. But what kind of general education should be provided?

Gradually, I began to formulate a radically new core curriculum in my mind. It contained team taught courses with professors from many disciplines. It was international, interdisciplinary, problem oriented, and issue based. It included cross-cultural courses treating rival political-economic systems; diplomatic history, comparative law, economics, religion, and philosophy; concepts of nationalism and revolution; the pro's and con's of technology; techniques and strategies for peace and disarmament; notions of progress and prejudice; the relation of politics to geography; the historical roots of modern problems; and the directions those problems might take in the future. A capstone course in interdependence would pull together these various threads of knowledge, and would feature outside speakers in diplomacy, foreign relations, and international trade. I got so excited over this curriculum, I could hardly sleep.

Then a marvelous thing happened. In another dream, Michael came back with the girl. "Doctor," he said, "in the last two weeks we've had a strange experience. I've taken this young woman across the country. Nobody gave any satisfactory answers. So I thought I'd give you a second chance." "Mike," I said, "I've got a curriculum that's gonna knock your wings off." And I told him about the problem-oriented approach. I told him about the cross-cultural courses and the team-taught techniques. As I talked, Mike began to glow all over. When I finished, he said, "By God! That's exactly what I'm looking for! We'll send this young woman to UB!" But at that euphoric moment the girl intervened. Emboldened by anticipation of her future status, she said, "Mr. President (I thought that was a nice touch, coming from her), the courses you've described are inspiring. But what makes you think the *faculty* would ever approve such a curriculum?" Again I was speechless. Again the angel took the girl by the hand, and walked away.

As this story suggests, many professors are part of the problem. To internationalize the core would require a radical reconstruction of the undergraduate curriculum. Most faculties do not have the temperament to make such extensive alterations. Individual faculty might be nonconformists, but when they act as a group, there are few organizations more resistant to change. Moving a faculty toward an internationalized core would be like moving a cemetery or picking up an elephant. It probably can be done, but no one has tried it yet.

Three universities—Gonzaga in Washington State, Central Michigan, and Florida International— made a bold effort along these lines in the early 1980's. Through symposia of academic, business, government, and media leaders, they conceptualized three thirty-six hour internationalized cores focusing on cross-cultural mobility, economic development, environment problems, regional conflicts, and interdependence of peoples. These outlines were strenuously debated at the 1984 International Association of University Presidents (IAUP) triennial conference in Bangkok. But then nothing happened. None of the prototype cores ever got introduced into the curricula of even the three institutions that sponsored the symposia!

Someday soon a college faculty is going to be bold enough to actually teach an internationalized core like the one described above. In anticipation of that event, I want to suggest five adjuncts to that curriculum. The first, a course on the environment, has already been described in Chapter 15. The second would be foreign language workshops using the "total immersion" process pioneered by John Rassias of Dartmouth College. Rassias, who began his career with me at UB, is a flamboyant Greek who will throw chairs out the window, pray on his knees, dress like Robespierre or Rabelais, or do anything else necessary to enthrall students with language. He once won a bet by teaching conversational Spanish to police in ten days. The languages emphasized here would be Spanish, Chinese, and Arabic, which is where the political, economic, and therefore linguistic action will be in the next decades.

The third adjunct to this internationalized core would be study abroad for at least one semester—preferably in Latin America, China, or the Middle East, while living with representative families in those regions. It was in paying tribute to this activity that President Eisenhower made one of his most admired comments. "It is governments that make war," he said, "and people who make peace." Through exchanges, every student can build a personal bridge of peace toward someone from another culture.

Jonathan Swift, the satirical author of *Gulliver's Travels*, once said that he hated the human race, but he loved Tom, Dick, and Harry. We might think we hate Germans, Russians, or Japanese. We might even make the grievous error of stereotyping these cultures. But then we meet Johan, Yuri, or Yoshio, and we realize they are not at all like what we thought. If we ever achieve world peace, we will realize in retrospect that it is nothing more than a collection of little "peaces," a mosaic of small friendships such as those which develop through student exchanges.

Each of us must start the peace process somewhere. For me, the process began in Tokyo, some years after I flew against the Japanese in China. The "Zero" fighter planes, with the Rising Sun emblem on their wings, had always invoked feelings of fear and, yes, even hatred in me. Then I found myself, as a young professor, at a Tokyo Rotary meeting. When we rose to salute the flag of Japan, I felt extreme discomfort. At least I would not have to sing their national anthem. After all, I could not read or speak Japanese. But my smiling host courteously passed me an English translation. I gulped, and sang. That was the beginning of a new kind of thinking on my part.

A further step in my own international development occurred in 1988. On a plane from Moscow to what was then Soviet Georgia, Ginny and I met Vladimir Tsotsilia, a Georgian author, who invited us to his home for dinner. He had never met an American, but his library shelves were stocked with American books, and his grandchildren had learned by heart every Michael Jackson song. Vladimir and his wife, Nina, had met in a prisoner of war camp in Germany, to which they were transported after being captured during World War II. Nina had been born in Leningrad, where her mother, brother, and sister starved to death during Hitler's brutal siege. Listening to them talk, I realized for the first time why Russians are so paranoid about their borders. They have been invaded repeatedly throughout history, most recently by Germany, and the people suffered terribly each time. A quarter of all the men in Georgia were killed during World War II.

During the evening, word got around the village that "Americans were in the house," and neighbors peered through the open door at the "Martians" from the West. When the time came to leave, the grandchildren brought out a small recorder and played Michael Jackson's "We Are the World," taped from a BBC broadcast. Everyone stood silently and listened. All of us, both American and Georgian, felt that something special was happening. We exchanged gifts—Ginny's was the shawl off her shoulders, Nina's a black Georgian vase, obviously an heirloom. We said goodbye, and went out into the cold night air, our hearts still warm with friendship. We had become one family in a single night, even though none of us ever saw each other again.

Study abroad, or at least inter-personal experience abroad, is crucial to developing a global perspective. A fourth adjunct to this international curriculum would be an internship with one of the non-governmental organizations (NGO's) attempting to save the earth or its inhabitants—e.g., the United Nations Association, Peace Action, Greenpeace, Save the Children, Economists Allied for Arms Reduction, Gun Control, Inc. This latter is of course domestic rather than international, but as a Japanese educator said to me in Kobe, Japan, in 1993, before hundreds of people, "If you care about violence so much, why don't you do something about it in your own country?"

Speaking of violence, when my children Chris and Greg were young, they wanted me to rebuild the "Christmas garden" that my father had built each holiday season. Mounted on planks and covered with moss and gravel to simulate grass and roads, the "garden" consisted of miniature trains, passengers waiting at stations, home and street lights, a number of "lakes" (pieces of glass surrounded by pebbles), waxed cloth mountains, shepherds, sheep, and of course a crèche with the baby Jesus and the Wise Men. Right next to the crèche my father always placed a fort, out of which were marching Buckingham Palace guards. They were peaceful chaps, with bugles and drums and an occasional rifle (unloaded, I am sure).

When my father died, all these materials were shipped to my home in Cincinnati—except for the guards, which somehow got lost in transit. My children were in tears. So I went down to a department store to find replacements. "I'm sorry," said the store clerk. "We don't carry the wooden guards anymore. What about a rubberized infantry combat team?" The team consisted of miniature soldiers on the attack, bayonets flashing and guns at the ready. The officer had been hit by a grenade, and was clutching his breast and falling, held up on his little rubber stand by the ingenuity of the manufacturer.

I tried to picture the combat team next to the crèche of the baby Jesus. Somehow it didn't seem right. So I built the garden without any military dimension that year, and wrote an article "My Son Won't Get Soldiers This Christmas," which appeared in *Family Circle* magazine. It was not my intention to oppose all military gifts to children, but simply to suggest that guns and soldiers did not seem appropriate on the birthday of the Prince of Peace. Since then, I've changed my mind—now I believe that military toys are an inappropriate gift for any occasion. A *New Yorker* cartoon got it right when it showed a smiling toy department clerk standing next to a huge sign which said, "This department is disarming: All toy guns 75% off!"

In addition to an environment course, foreign language, study abroad, and an NGO internship, an international curriculum should contain a workshop on peacemaking, keeping in mind that tomorrow's wars are always fought by today's students. The main function of this workshop on peacemaking would be to counter the "Rambo" mentality of the mass media, and the war orientation of much traditional history, by emphasizing peace activists like Mahatma Gandhi, Martin Luther King, Oscar Arias, Albert Schweitzer, the Dalai Lama, and Alva Myrdahl. The challenge here would be to make peace heroes as exciting as their war counterparts. As Colman McCarthy wrote in *The Rotarian* for September 1996, "We are taught about those who conquered opposing armies, but not about those who conquered hate, injustice, and poverty. We are taught about those who practice violence, but not about those who won victories through non-violence. Let's give peace a place in the curriculum of every school in the world."

This kind of international curriculum, which combines a world view with the job adaptability of the liberal arts core, will be pre-requisite to achieving any kind of professional success in the 21st Century, let alone any kind of maturity as a modern citizen. This is so because inter-dependence is now a reality, and economics is its base. Since World War II, American exports and assets abroad have exploded into the hundreds of billions, while foreign investments in the United States have likewise increased exponentially.

Some faculty might not be aware of the above, but corporate leaders are. Victor Kiam, who liked the Remington shaver so much that he bought the company, says this about future managers: "In the next decade, CEO's will need to have a global perspective. They'll no longer be able to say, 'My only competition is in Milwaukee.' They'll have to ask, 'What's going on in Hong Kong?'" A recent survey conducted by Korn-Ferry International and Columbia University's School of Business comes to the same conclusion. The executives interviewed agreed that the "global village" will become a reality, and that there will be a shortage of executives qualified to deal with unpredictable economic fluctuations and rapid technological change. "In a world where you will have to turn on a dime, flexibility and adaptability to lead the firm and to deal with crisis will be essential," says Robert Slater of Korn-Ferry. Slater stresses that top managers will need to know several languages and comparative economics. They will also need exceptional interpersonal and communication skills that cross national boundaries.

In the last analysis, the aim of an internationalized liberal arts core is to change the way people think. To create a new mentality. Einstein was once asked what the scientific antidote was to the bomb. He replied, "There is no scientific antidote; the only antidote is education. You've got to change the way people think." Especially would the proposed curriculum give us a chance to destroy stereotypes before it is too late. Remember the story by Ray Bradbury of the astronaut who got off a space ship and saw a spider coming toward him? The spider was 15 feet high, with hairy legs and bulging eyes; he was smiling, but the astronaut was so terrified he didn't notice. He took out his ray gun and killed the spider because he had a stereotyped concept of what spiders are. But this spider was part of a super race, far more intelligent than humans. In revenge, thousands of giant spiders descended on earth and destroyed it. From this fictitious disaster we can hopefully learn that cultures which seem initially repellent might in fact be beautiful when better known.

Through international education we can promote survival. Colleges should strive with all the skills at their command to develop graduates who will give civilization a chance to continue. H.G. Wells has given us a clear warning. "Human history," he said, "becomes more and more a race between education and catastrophe." The chief motivation of an international curriculum must be to help education win that race, against war and for peace. Rodrigo Carazo, former president of Costa Rica, speaks more bluntly. "If you want peace, educate for peace." In other words, before we can disarm nations, we must "disarm" the minds of their citizens. In this sense, every college should be a University for Peace, not just in what and how it teaches, but in the behavior of its faculty and administrators toward each other, and toward their students. Teaching peace by example is a moral act, and carries far more weight than words.

16

To Conform or Not Conform

Our six-year-old daughter Chris (perhaps at our urging?)
had toddled upstairs and jumped on his stomach with both feet.

A
S WE ENTER THE 21st Century, problems of peace have become so
vast and complex that they cry
out for bold and imaginative leadership. But to solve such problems, democratic leaders must get ahead of their electorate, and once they do,
they risk losing their constituency and their office. The dilemma here is
conforming or not conforming, and it confronts both leaders and citizens.

Under these circumstances, one of the obligations colleges must
undertake is to orient their students to the political world, through convocation programs, off-campus internships, or through social science
courses or clubs. At a minimum, students, regardless of major, should
be given the opportunity to learn about the various types of governmental systems, the historical roots of political parties here and abroad,
the relation of such parties to the "liberal" and "conservative" traditions,
the interaction between domestic and foreign policy, and the risks and
rewards of conformance versus non-conformance, especially the relation of the latter to the law and the rights of society.

Albert Parker, the first college president I worked for, once said that
a liberal is a young man who tells conservatives how to spend their
money. His comment suggests that young people begin as liberals and

become conservatives as they grow older. Yet national surveys of freshmen over the last decade reveal that a majority consider themselves conservatives! In fact, self-styled conservative newspapers like the Dartmouth, Princeton, and California *Reviews* are popular on many campuses as alternatives to allegedly liberal papers supported by college administrations.

One problem we all have, whether in college or not, is deciding what political camp we are in. That is not easy nowadays, because the labels overlap. The root of "liberal" is the Latin "liber," meaning free. Thus a liberal is supposedly one who is free from provincialism, from prejudice, from the past. The problem is that many conservatives feel the same way. Likewise, the root of "conservative" is the Latin "conservare," to guard or protect, retain. But the true conservative does not want to retain what is bad, any more than the true liberal wants to change what is good. Hence the difference between these two great traditions might be more a matter of emphasis than of principle. In any event, the genius of the American system is that both parties contain advocates for both approaches.

I once unexpectedly sat down next to Eric Severeid, the former TV commentator, in an Aspen sauna. We had met before, but not in the buff. After the initial embarrassment wore off, we got into a discussion on national politics. Severeid revealed that Franklin Roosevelt and Wendell Wilkie had corresponded on realigning the political parties. Roosevelt would take all the liberals into his party, and Wilkie all the conservatives into his. The idea was to give voters a choice. Severeid thought it was a bad idea. As he saw it, the mixture of ideology in both parties provides us with a stability lacking in many other political systems. To that I replied, "Eric, if both ideologies are in both parties, what is the difference between them?" He became quiet for a bit, deep in thought. Then he looked up, grinned, and said, "Maybe the biggest difference is that one's in and one's out."

On another memorable occasion, I got the same answer from a professional politician. Rosalind Carter was in town, and the Bridgeport mayor suggested a dinner for her at Waldemere,UB's official residence, as we had done for a Republican notable the prior month. The event was a nerve-wracking experience, as Secret Service agents swarmed into Waldemere and expelled everyone but Ginny and me. They even assigned us the code names "Eagle" and "Dove." At one point during the preparations, I overheard an agent whisper into his walkie-talkie, "Eagle now moving toward bathroom." There is a certain thrill in being referred to in such a manner, even for such a destination.

When Rosalind and her escorts arrived, one of the luminaries (actually the party treasurer) joked about my "independent" status. "Why don't you raise funds for us, son?" he queried lightly. "Frankly," I replied, "I don't understand the difference between the parties. Educate me." "Well," he chuckled, "the biggest difference is that one's in and one's out. If the in's want to stay in, they've got to raise more money than the out's." Before he could continue this learned treatise, the phone rang, and my young assistant answered. An austere voice came over the line saying, "This is the White House. We must speak immediately with the president's wife." To which my aide replied, "*Which* president's wife, Miles's or Carter's?" What a joy to have such assistants! I gave the young man a raise the next month.

Regardless of party affiliations, liberals tend to emphasize the concerns of the individual rather than those of society, and are therefore thought to be more nonconformist than conservatives. But here we are back in the soup again, because Albert Parker, my first president and an ardent conservative, was also a non-conformist of the first rank. When he walked on campus, in a battered hat and rumpled coat, he liked to grab the trunks of young trees and swing around them several times. If you were trying to talk to him, you had to get a few words in as he passed by on each swing. He once embarrassed an audience of students and faculty by saying he knew the campus trees better than he knew them. He probably did. He had personally planted several thousand, and preferred them to people because they didn't talk.

Parker aside, there are two kinds of nonconformity—fake and genuine. The fake nonconformist (like some of the Beat Generation) looks *outside* himself and then does the opposite of what everyone else is doing. The most memorable fake I can remember was Peter Viereck, a poet from Mount Holyoke College, who was invited to participate in the Hanover College literary series. When I met him at the airport, he wore a business suit and seemed to be reasonably conventional. But when he came down for dinner that night, he had costumed himself in a green eyeshade and a rumpled sweater, so oversized that only his fingertips protruded from the sleeves. Oblivious to his hosts, he brought a copy of *Saturday Review* to the table and proceeded to read throughout the meal. Finally Ginny, who did not suffer rudeness kindly, got his attention. "Tell me Mr. Viereck," she inquired, "does your wife mind your reading magazines at dinner?" "Divorced," he responded cryptically, and went on reading.

As dessert was served, I managed to distract him again for a few seconds. "The students will be arriving soon for your presentation," I said. At that he leapt up and gasped, "Too tired," stumbled upstairs, and threw himself across the guest bed. He returned shortly to join the students, and we thought it was because he felt guilty about his behavior. We discovered the real reason later. Our six-year-old daughter Chris (perhaps at our urging?) had toddled upstairs and jumped on his stomach with both feet. When he left campus two mornings later, he was once again attired in his business suit, his poet's costume packed, awaiting the next lecture series. It had all been an act, put on by a charter member of the cult of pseudo-Bohemia.

Colleges should help students to perceive and appreciate genuine and therefore useful nonconformity. In contrast to the fake, a genuine non-conformist like Robert Frost looks *within* himself and does what his conscience dictates, regardless of what others say or do. When Frost was a student at Amherst, he was considered for a fraternity, but the members were suspicious of his love for nature. At one point, a fraternity brother accosted him and asked, "What do you do out there in the woods, anyway?" "I gnaw the bark off trees," Frost replied. He never made the pledge class.

A more controversial type of non-conformity is that which breaks the law. As Justice Abe Fortes once said, everybody has a *moral* right to break the law, but nobody has a *legal* right to do so. Those who oppose the law on grounds of conscience, Fortes advised, should not assume the world will come round to their side, as it did for Ghandi and Martin Luther King. Society has a right to protect itself. Jefferson was on the mark when he wrote, "We are a nation of laws, not of men," and "There can be no liberty except liberty under the law." What Jefferson was saying, and what colleges should teach their students, is that *the freedom to non-conform is not absolute.*

At Alfred during the 1960's, the Students for a Democratic Society (SDS) led escalating demonstrations which interfered with teaching, denied students entry to classes, threatened to burn buildings (especially the venerated but wholly wooden Alumni Hall), and ultimately disrupted the annual ROTC review. Midway through these incidents, and after much reflection, I issued a "Policy on Demonstrations," the heart of which was a quotation attributed to Oliver Wendell Holmes: "In a democracy, you have the right to swing your elbows in a crowd; but that right ends when your elbow touches the other fellow's nose." In short, nobody has the right to disrupt another person's rights. Sure, the SDS had a right to demonstrate against ROTC, but not in a way which disrupted the cadets' right to their own demonstration.

Somehow the SDS leaders never grasped this fundamental principle. When the ROTC review began, they raced among the cadets, who thankfully never broke ranks. Angry parents and alumni started coming down from the stands, shaking their fists and yelling threats at the "radicals." Alfred's police force consisted of four pot-bellied elders, straight out of the chorus of *The Pirates of Penzance*. Had a fight started, they never could have stopped it.

Later, after due process, I expelled the SDS leaders. They retaliated by taking the University to Federal District Court in Buffalo, and then on to the Second Circuit Court of Appeals in New York. They claimed that in expelling them, Alfred had violated their First Amendment rights of free speech and free assembly. Justice Friendly wrote the Appeals Court verdict which began, "First Amendment rights were indeed violated. The rights violated were those of the cadets and parents." All right! The Olean (New York) newspaper came out with a banner headline which read, "Adults Win One at Alfred!" "Powe vs. Miles" as it was called became a "moot court" case for many American law schools.

One part of getting educated is learning when to conform, and when not to. We conform by obeying traffic signals, because we need mutual self-protection. We conform to the conventions of spelling to assure reciprocal communication. In both cases, we follow these conventions to avoid social chaos, not because there's any logic to them. English spelling has been in a hopeless state for centuries, and as for traffic lights, why can't green mean "stop"? If there are times to conform to avoid anarchy, there are also times to defy convention as a matter of necessity. At a banquet once, I saw a guest spit out a mouthful of scorching baked potato. As his face flushed and his eyes watered, he gasped, "You know, some dammed fools would have swallowed that!"

The most necessary time to non-conform, from a moral viewpoint, is when we have finally backed up to the hard core of our individual consciences. We have accepted compromises and attempted reconciliations, but the main issue, even with the differences narrowed, still remains at odds with our inner self. In such situations we have no moral alternative but to declare with Luther, "Here I stand!" However, *how* we make that declaration will determine how tolerantly our audience receives it. Through Speech, Communication, or some other general education requirement, colleges should teach students how to get their ideas across, even when the listeners have different views.

Confronting a hostile audience is dangerous business. Some years ago in Missouri, I directly attacked the segregation of blacks and whites, even though I knew the audience opposed integration. When I got into the host's car after the lecture to go to the reception, we headed instead for the airport. "What about the reception?" I asked. "It's been canceled," he snapped. Obviously, the only thing I had accomplished was to enrage my audience. The next time I spoke to Southerners, I tried a different, and smarter, tack. I told a humorous story from Harry Golden's *Only in America.*

According to Harry, there was an old black man who inherited an ancient car from an uncle. He had never driven before, so the first thing he did was to drive into Nashville and go through a red light. A policeman stopped him and said, "I have to give you a ticket. Do you have anything to say?" "Yes," said the offender. "I seen all the white folks going through the green light, I figured the red light was for us Negroes." The audience hesitated, then burst into laughter and applause. This time the reception following was not canceled. And further, *they got my point.*

Emerson declares in the essay *Self-Reliance* that all of us become conformists as we grow older. I can tell you sadly that to some degree Emerson is right. None of us will ever again have the freedom to non-conform that we enjoyed as undergraduates in college. Many parents, forgetting their own youthful nonconformity, are shocked and bewildered when their student offspring return home for their first holiday break and express wildly different views from theirs. How did these children, raised in a conventional household, suddenly become flaming radicals? Are the faculty a bunch of pinkos? Probably not. The free-thinking of college students exists partly because colleges are tolerant, partly because campuses revel in debate over competing ideas, and partly because, as Emerson said, "It is easy to non-conform when we are sure of our supper." Students who are largely supported by their parents as well as their colleges can enjoy the luxury of being radical. It is another matter when they must pay their own bills.

As a case in point, the expulsion of the Alfred students who disrupted the ROTC review occurred only a few weeks before graduation. To protest, SDS seniors carried all sorts of signs, and wore all sorts of outlandish clothes, as they participated in the commencement ceremonies. One bearded fellow was completely nude beneath his robe. As he approached me on stage to receive his diploma, he suddenly "flashed" his birthday suit, first at me and then the audience. I was amazed to note that he had painted Mercurochrome around his nipples. I suppose this was intended to shock me, and quite frankly, it did.

A year later I was speaking in Boston. It was not a University event, but some alumni came to listen in. At the end of my speech, they trooped up to the platform to say hello. One of them was especially well dressed —neatly pressed three-piece suit, modest two-color shirt with an Edwardian collar, conservative tie, brightly shined shoes, and so on. He extended his hand for a cordial handshake. I looked at him closely. "You know," I said, "you look familiar. You couldn't be the guy with the Mercurochrome . . .?" My voice trailed off. "Yes sir," he grinned "Sure am." "I can't understand it," I said. "One year ago you were bearded, defiant and nude. Now you're shaven, respectful, and dressed. How explain the change?" "Oh, it's very simple, Doctor," he said. "I'm in the business world now. It's a whole new ball game!"

As the story of the Mercurochrome Man suggests, there is enormous pressure to conform in any society. If you attempt to defy the conventions of your community, society will, as Emerson warned, "whip you for your non-conformity." I can speak from personal experience on this point. As mentioned in the Prologue, the prevailing view at Juniata College, during my student days, was that dancing was evil. In rebuttal, I wrote an editorial for the student newspaper, arguing that dancing was in fact "morally neutral," and that the "folk games" indulged in by Juniata students looked suspiciously like dancing. The editor-in-chief had said in advance that she would not censor my column. But she added that she would fire me if I "came out" with such views. I thought she was kidding. She wasn't. I lost my job as news editor of the college newspaper over this issue. Despite several efforts, I was not let back on the paper until my senior year, when I was given the humiliating assignment of writing the weekly "Tomahawk" gossip column.

If I were a college president again, I would give this advice, learned the hard way, to graduating seniors and other incipient leaders. If you must defy the crowd, in college or out, pick a principle that you feel deeply about, *get your facts straight in advance*, and then try for the most favorable timing. Even then, prepare to be ridiculed at first, as Joseph Lister was, and maybe punished disproportionately for your stand. Despite hostility, always act peacefully, never impugn the character of your opponents, and never violate the rights of others who hold different views. And yes, as a potential leader don't expect to be vindicated any time soon. In my case, I was lucky enough to achieve vindication, eventually. Juniata has dancing now. They don't even call it folk games anymore.

17

Leaders Need Followers

She put one end of her ear trumpet into her ear,
and the other end in front of the guest's mouth.

I N THE MINDS of college seniors, leadership is always associated with commencement, because commencement speakers always talk about college grads as future leaders. Actually, anyone who has conducted as many graduation ceremonies as I have knows that a leader must first and foremost learn to confront emergencies, and that there is no time like commencement to test his mettle. In Chapter 3, I described the senior commandos who turned 6,000 seats around. In my days on the commencement platform, I've also had to grab an electronically controlled lectern that suddenly moved under its own power; dry off an honorary degree candidate who got drenched when the awning above him broke, just as I was saying, "So I now confer upon you . . ."; chase after an academic procession that was meekly following an absent-minded Grand Marshal into the men's room; and comfort a dean who testified that the speaker had "perverted" technology, when he meant "perfected" (far from ignoring the error, the seniors applauded enthusiastically).

One problem with commencement speakers is that they put too much emphasis on leadership. Nobody can be a leader in everything; everybody must be a follower in some areas. The scarcity of good followers is illustrated by the tale of a student who applied to Vassar. Her father wrote a supporting letter conceding that his daughter was not a leader, but emphasizing that she was a discerning and astute follower. A few days later the father received a phone call from the Vassar admissions director. "Mr. Jones," the director said, "Your daughter is unique in my experience. So far this year we have received 857 applications from leaders. Your daughter is the only follower who has applied. We desperately need some followers around here, Mr. Jones. Tell your daughter we welcome her to Vassar."

The qualities of a good follower, especially discernment and knowledge of the issues, are as important as those of a good leader. Followers should expect their viewpoints to be considered seriously by those they support, but should appreciate that leaders must often choose from among many conflicting options or persuasions. Stewart McKinney, a conscientious Congressman from southwestern Connecticut, once sent a questionnaire to all his constituents, seeking their views on public policy matters. He explained that all of the answers would be computerized, so that he would know exactly how the majority of constituents wanted him to vote on any given issue. I phoned Stewart to ask for clarification. Was the questionnaire simply for consultation? If so, fine. I was pleased that he would like to hear my views and those of others. Or was he going to vote in accord with the computerized results? If so, not so fine. After all, if he was going to vote exactly as his constituents indicated, then we needn't pay for him to exercise judgment in Washington. We could simply program his computer so that it would spit out the district's vote at each Congressional roll call.

As Thomas Jefferson saw it, leaders should do what they think is right for the country, not what they think will be popular with 51 percent of their constituents. In retrospect, the most admired leaders have been those who had a clear scale of values, and who refused to deviate from the higher principles of that scale, no matter how many people they angered. A cardinal case here is Harry Truman. When he became President after Franklin Roosevelt's death, I feared for the future of America. Here was a former haberdasher, a "machine" politician who used vulgar language and never went to college. What I didn't know until later was that he had read almost every book in Independence, Missouri, and had amassed a collection of historical works in his own library. You could open any of his books to almost any page, as I later did, and find annotations by this future President of the United States. He was like those rare "self-educated" people whom I discussed in the first chapter of this book.

By the time I went to Independence some years later for a lecture commitment, my views about Harry had changed. I asked for and was granted an interview. Out of office and aging by then, he entered the room slowly on the arm of a black Army sergeant. But his blue eyes twinkled. "Sir," I said, during the course of our conversation, "what was your most important decision?" I assumed he would refer to his anti-Communist intervention in Korea, or his moves to support civil rights, or, most likely, the dropping of the atom bomb on Hiroshima which ended World War II. But he didn't say any of those things. Instead he replied, "The release of General MacArthur." Note the delicate use of "release" rather than "firing"—and this from a man noted for blunt expletives! When I looked shocked, he smiled and said, "Let me explain. General MacArthur was one of the greatest military geniuses of all time. He was greater than. . . ." At this point he swept back to Alexander the Great and Hannibal; came up through history to Kings Alfred and Charlemagne; briefly touched on Wellington, Nelson and Napoleon; and in two minutes ended by noting assorted heroes of later wars. Then he took a breath and said, "So why did I release him, if he was greater than any of those commanders?"

By this time I was on the edge of my seat. "Yes sir," I said. "That's the point. Why did you?" "Because what was at stake was civilian control of the military," he said. He paused a long time, looked me in the eye, put his hand on my arm, and said quietly, "Don't ever forget, young man, the essence of democracy is civilian control." I was stunned. I had read a number of political theorists, e.g., John Locke, James Fenimore Cooper, Alexis de Tocqueville. They had said that the essence of democracy was equality before the law, or the right to elect one's own legislators, or whatever. But I had never heard Truman's definition. On reflection, I concluded he was right. Without civilian control, none of the other qualities of democracy matters much.

However, the point is not whether Truman was right or wrong. The point is that he held a conviction so strongly that he would not back away from it, even if it meant firing the most admired general in America. On this matter of conscience, he was prepared to risk not only his popularity, but also his historical reputation. In the short term, it appeared that he had lost both. The editorial press was furious, his fellow politicians had apoplexy, and the public vented their outrage. In revenge, they all joined to give the returning MacArthur the most tumultuous ticker-tape parade in New York history. But in the history books, look where Truman stands now!

Truman did not compromise on the issue of civilian control, but he did compromise on many other issues. As noted elsewhere, there is nothing morally wrong with compromise (or "accommodation" as it is called today), up to the point where it impinges on one's integrity, conscience, or duty. Anyone who has ever tried to lead large organizations, whether universities, corporations, or the country, recognizes that compromise on major issues is justified on at least three counts: first, nothing will happen without it, because followers want to feel some "ownership" in any impending decision; second, if they do not sense that ownership, they will not support the policy; and third, the assorted views of the "collective mind" encompass far more good ideas than can be conceived by a single individual, no matter how brilliant. In fact, compromise, up to the point of conscience, is a sign of the "open mind" discussed in Chapter 13. To reject all but our own thoughts is to play God, as the political science professor did in that chapter.

We should sympathize with those at the top, because they often must compromise between unacceptable alternatives. They are in the same predicament as the church warden who saw Miss Dugan suddenly fall from the balcony. Her dress caught on a chandelier and she hung upside down screaming, her lower (now upper) extremities uniquely revealed. The minister, who knew how to address an emergency when he saw one, yelled out, "The first man to lay eyes on poor Miss Dugan will be struck blind." The warden put both hands over his eyes, thought for a moment, and then said to his companion, "Well maybe so. But I'm going to risk one eye, anyway."

In my experience, most good leaders want honest advice, even if it irritates them at the outset. Some years ago I called a meeting at UB to announce a plan which had been developed over many months in consultation with a distinguished group of people. At the meeting, a new staff member, Bill Flynn, joined us for the first time. As I described the "final" plan, he grew increasingly restless and apprehensive. Finally he raised his hand, stood up, and spoke nervously with obvious reluctance. "I haven't been in on any of the earlier meetings," Bill said. "So maybe I've missed something. But it seems to me. . . ." He then identified several major flaws in the plan. When he finished, there was an embarrassed silence. Everyone knew he was right. As for myself, I was extremely annoyed. I had devoted months of emotional and mental energy to this document. And now this guy was coming out of nowhere and blowing it out of the water. But the plan went back to the drawing board and was radically revised. Leaders need followers like Bill Flynn, to keep them from going off the deep end.

Regardless of style, the purpose of communication, at least from a leader's viewpoint, is to persuade, inspire, and motivate. Of course the leader wishes to inform his followers of his viewpoint. Of course he wants to convince them of the rightness of his view. But most of all, he seeks to motivate them to move in his direction. Thus communication is the glue which binds the follower to the leader. But the glue will not hold unless the leader has a vision which inspires people to passionately support him. Martin Luther King communicated not just because he was eloquent, but because he had a vision which inspired the black man and shamed the white.

In the last analysis vision is more important than eloquence A great vision will somehow make itself felt even if poorly articulated, just as a great personality will somehow transcend an ugly face or body. The Greek philosopher Demosthenes stuttered. Churchill had a similar speech impediment. Eleanor Roosevelt was painfully awkward and plain as a poke. Yet, all of them carried the day with their visions: Demosthenes, of a Greek state; Churchill, of victory over the Nazis; Mrs. Roosevelt, of the dignity of women and the disadvantaged. Despite the physical barriers, their messages got through.

It might be helpful to compare communication to a pipe and vision to water. Without water flowing through the pipe, the pipe is empty, useless, meaningless. An empty pipe never turned anybody on—or off. In short, the leader must have something to say; otherwise, there is nothing to communicate, and therefore no followers to be inspired. One thinks of the famous anecdote in Henry David Thoreau's *Walden*. Thoreau was giving a party for a famous deaf woman. A guest insisted on meeting the woman, and Thoreau finally brought him into the presence of the great lady. She put one end of her ear trumpet into her ear, and the other end in front of the guest's mouth. Only then did the guest suddenly realize that he had nothing to say! To his credit, he remained silent. Unfortunately, most people who have nothing to say talk anyway.

Until recently, colleges showed no interest in leadership as an academic subject. They simply assumed, with the commencement speakers, that college automatically produces leaders, even though some graduates (including Yale's) wind up on the Bowery. The first college to formally place "leadership" in the curriculum was probably Mount St. Mary's in Los Angeles, which announced a "Leadership Program" in 1975. Other institutions prominent in the field today include Gettysburg College in Pennsylvania, Wartburg College in Iowa, Duke University in North Carolina, and the University of Richmond in Virginia.

At Wartburg College, two million has been raised for endowed chairs in leadership, applied ethics, and international studies. The leadership emphasis is on mentoring—students "shadow" business and political leaders, observing how they handle responsibility and struggle to honor commitments. At Duke University in Durham, the emphasis is on field work in famine-stricken Africa, Durham soup kitchens, and rural Florida ghettos. At the University of Richmond, a twenty million dollar gift has created the Jepson Institute of Leadership Studies, where the emphasis is on the scholar/activist, the unity of knowing and doing. In 1992, Richmond became the first liberal arts college to offer a bachelor's degree in leadership.

Today there are around 800 colleges offering some form or variant of leadership studies, ranging from a single course to a major or minor. Academic credit in the subject is also offered at free-standing institutes such as the Center for Creative Leadership in Greensboro, and the International Leadership Center at Dallas. Some of these efforts have attracted the interest of foundations and corporations, including the W.K. Kellogg Foundation in Battle Creek, Michigan.

Some schools have cobbled together anything that sounds remotely relevant, and have called it a "leadership program." Others have shown considerable skill in drawing on resources already on campus—for example, counseling and conflict management workshops run by the student affairs department; organizational behavior seminars offered by the business college; presidential and public policy courses run by the political scientists; applied ethics taught by the philosophy department; advanced communication and speech drawn from English or similar units; and community problems as identified by the city government.

In the words of one college catalogue, all such activities seek "to cultivate selflessness, passionate commitment, and civic conscience." A general leadership course should be an elective part of the liberal arts core, and therefore available to all students regardless of major.

It is ironic that some college faculty are showing interest in teaching leadership, at the very time when trustees are leaning toward "managers" rather than leaders to head their institutions. Beset by mounting fiscal and enrollment problems, many trustees are insisting that managerial abilities be uppermost in any search profile for a new president. There is of course nothing wrong with seeking managers; they are valuable and often devoted types for any institution. But a manager, by temperament and function, cannot be a leader; while a leader, if given adequate help in his weaker capacities, can handle many managerial responsibilities.

It might be helpful to identify these different functions, both for faculty who are teaching leadership, and for trustees who are seeking managers. To start with, the leader is macro and the manager is micro. The first is responsible for the whole organization; the second, for only a part of it. This difference influences all of the other differences. For example, the two types make decisions in different ways. Given a specific problem, the manager waits until all the facts are in before attempting a judgment. The leader is more aware of the time factor. If he waits until all the facts are in, his competitor might pass him by. So he assembles a reasonable degree of evidence, then acts on intuition, leaping forward while his competitor is still pondering the issue.

Because of their devotion to data, managers tend to play it safe. They act only within what they perceive to be the political possibilities. The leader is, of course, mindful of politics in the broad sense. But he is also adept at brinkmanship. He is willing to take a risk for principle, if he thinks it important for his institution, and if he believes he has a good shot at success. By contrast, the manager looks on brinkmanship with dismay, and failure resulting from it as a disaster. The leader, on the other hand, sees failure with a sense of humor and perspective. Yes, failure is embarrassing, but it's also a vehicle for learning what not to do the next time. So the leader picks himself up, dusts off his business suit, and cheerfully tries another approach to the problem.

To sum up, leaders are pathfinders. Either they persuade others to follow them into uncharted territory, or they lead people back home when they get lost. It is a temptation here to name names, but I will let readers cite their own favorite examples from history, academic life, the modern corporate world, and elsewhere. A possible synonym for "pathfinder" is "change agent." Leaders usually want to change things. They are anti-status quo. Those who favor the status quo perceive leaders as rebels, reformers, even revolutionaries. But to be a revolutionary, that is a *successful* rebel, one must adjust to the possible. Banging one's head against a wall is not the best way to advance a cause.

Nathaniel Greene, Washington's most trusted general, knew that his rabble army was no match in open battle for Cornwallis' disciplined troops. So he adjusted to what was possible. Like the North Vietnam nationalists two centuries later, he ordered his men to hit and run, hit and run. Later he allegedly said, "We have become experts at running. We will run in any direction, but preferably away from the enemy." The rattled Cornwallis chased Greene through the Virginia forests for six months, losing large numbers of redcoats to disease or desertion. Eventually he outran his own supply lines, and, like a dazed and wounded bull, finally surrendered to Washington at Yorktown. In the spirit of Nathaniel Greene, all would-be leaders should embrace and repeat nightly Reinhold Niebuhr's prayer: "Lord, give me the patience to endure what cannot be changed, the courage to change what can be changed, and the wisdom to know the one from the other."

Apart from managers versus leaders and status quo-ites versus rebels, let me express a few respectful reservations concerning the emergence of college-level leadership programs. The emphasis of such programs, especially in schools which offer a minor or major in the subject, is almost wholly on leadership. But the behavior of leaders, at least in a democracy, is driven by the aggressiveness or apathy of followers. Shouldn't some students aim to be followers, just like the young woman at Vassar? Why not a Follower Institute on some campus? In any event, leadership studies should avoid treating the leader in a vacuum. Instead, the effort should be made to analyze the leader's *relationship* to his followers, and vice versa, from a historical, psychological, and ethical perspective.

It is doubtful whether anyone should set out consciously to be a leader, any more than we should set out deliberately to be happy. Both goals, so sought, might be as elusive as Maeterlinck's bluebird. If we eventually become leaders, it is probably because we have done good work somewhere and someone has noticed. Or maybe we just got lucky.

One of the early books my mother gave me was *A Little Night Music* by Gerald Johnson of the *Baltimore Sun*. In the chapter "The Art of Coming In," he makes fun of himself, as an amateur cellist playing with a string quartet, for never "coming in" at the right time. Transferring this experience to history, Johnson argues that most leaders do not control the flow of events. They just have the knack or luck to be in the right place at the right time. To this view we could reply: "Yes, but don't they have the innate or learned leadership skills to know what to do when they get there?"

Another implication, in some leadership studies programs, is that one needs to be famous or become famous to be a leader. On the contrary, inspired teachers are among the most important leaders in America, just as curious students are among the most important followers. Rosa Parks, who refused to give up her seat on the Montgomery, Alabama, bus in 1955, started the civil rights movement. She was always thought of as a follower of Martin Luther King. But without her, he might never have had his chance. King had been busy building a constituency, but it was Rosa's courage that ignited the civil rights movement. So in this situation, who was the leader and who the follower?

A final reservation, where "leadership" is taught, is the assumption that leaders are made, not born. But what about John Major? His parents were circus workers, and he had no university training in leadership or anything else. Yet he rose to be Chancellor of the Exchequer (equivalent to Secretary of the Treasury in the U.S.), and eventually Prime Minister of Great Britain. If leaders can be "made," some of the making must certainly occur through experience outside college or before college studies begin.

As Chairman of the Ettinger Scholarship Committee of the Educational Foundation of America, I had the privilege of interviewing each year the final twelve high school candidates for two $50,000 scholarships. These candidates were required to supply, as a departure point for their interviews, brief essays on "The Most Meaningful Experience" in their high school years. Let me quote from an essay by a recent applicant, Judith Eve Johnson of Norwalk High School. "My goal has been to become a responsible leader. As class officer, I have learned the necessity for compromise. Take for example the Junior Prom. The colors, theme, and music selected were not my first choices. But I learned that for something to run smoothly, compromise is a key factor in any project's success."

And from Mary Beth Fitzgerald, also of Norwalk: "The most challenging experience of my career to date has been acting as captain of the cheerleading squad. To those unfamiliar with the inner workings of cheerleading, being captain may appear to be the job for a pony-tailed idiot. [But] the captain's role as a leader is to rise above all the squad divisiveness, and to create a spirit of unity. I must try to discourage 'star performers' who stir ill will among jealous peers. I am constantly trying to make the members see the squad as a whole, not as an arena for solo ambitions . . . I now know that I will be meeting difficult people all my life."

It looks like we have a couple of nascent leaders here. They probably started learning leadership in kindergarten, or maybe they had the ability from birth, or both. There is an analogy here with poetry. Nobody can teach a student to be a poet. But if the innate ability is there, teaching might refine or enhance or expand it. In short, everything we know about leadership suggests that its sources are an amalgam of birth, temperament, experience, study, occupation, and luck. It is this mix, each part proportioned differently in each case, that determines each leader's distinctive style—that is, each leader's distinctive way of communicating with his real or potential followers.

18

Leadership Styles

*If the man got nervous and said, "Well what about $10,000?",
Parker would say "Ah!"*

LEADERS DO NOT share any one leadership style, because they differ so much from one another. C.P. Snow's *Variety of Men* treats a number of leaders, regretfully all male, but helpful in addressing the subject. As the title suggests, they represent an incredible variety: one was a scientist, one a statesman, one a poet, one a public servant, and so on. Some were courageous, some timid; some belligerent, some loving; some short, some tall; some healthy, some sickly; some authoritarian, some democratic. Only one trait do these varied leaders have in common, namely the power to communicate. And of course, communication is the chief vehicle by which leaders project their leadership style.

When we examine Snow's leaders more carefully, we should not be surprised to find that they communicated in different ways. Some like Albert Schweitzer communicated by example. His hospital for Africans, and his loving attention to their illnesses, said more about his veneration for life than any theological work ever could. We think in this connection of Mother Teresa. She had no office, gave no commands, and lived in poverty. Yet she had more power than any parliament. "When you were with her," said an observer, "you almost had to wear sunglasses.

She radiated, and so did every dying or diseased person she touched." In recent times the leader who has most communicated by example has been Anwar Sadat of Egypt. No one today remembers what he *said* in Jerusalem, at the beginning of the Middle East peace process some years ago. But everyone remembers that he *went* there, at great personal and political risk. He did more than talk peace, he acted peace. Emerson's observation is appropriate. "What you are speaks so loud, I cannot hear what you say."

On the other hand (there's our old friend again!), Dag Hammarskjöld communicated chiefly by listening and reacting. So often we identify communication, especially the communication of a leader, with oratory. We gather to hear the leader give a speech. Presumably we listen, applaud, are inspired, and then rush out and do the leader's bidding. But this is monologue. A higher form of communication is dialogue. It is not the communication of a commander ordering his troops, but a sharing of ideas among equals in an atmosphere of mutual respect. Even dialogue fails to communicate if the parties involved are not on the same "wave length." There's the tale of the talkative girl and the deaf boy. She *talks* to him about her love and he *signs* to her about his. But neither can understand the other, so all love is lost between them. Dag Hammarskjöld was on everybody's wavelength. He understood and reacted appreciatively to what others said. He was able to do this because he was a truly humble person.

Benjamin Franklin's draft *Autobiography* listed twelve virtues, with a brief description of each. Someone pointed out that he had omitted the virtue of humility. Accordingly, Ben reluctantly added humility as the thirteenth virtue, and wrote underneath it this brief description. "It is not important to be humble, but it is extremely important to have the *appearance* of humility." As Ben grew older, he learned to use his version of humility as a way of communicating, that is, as a way of influencing people. Instead of telling members of the Philadelphia Assembly that they were stupid (as he had done when he was younger), he began to praise them for their erudition. But simultaneously he suggested that perhaps a different course of action, namely Ben's course, was better in this or that particular instance. To his delight, they agreed!

Some leaders, like Ben, only pretend to be humble. Others truly feel they can lead best by coming down among their followers, and sharing common experiences with them. Typical of this type is His

Majesty, King Bhumibol Adulvadej of Thailand. Despite fifty years of rule, making him the world's senior head of state, he still hands out diplomas to every college graduate. Frequently he is seen descending from a helicopter in the furthest reaches of the kingdom. Wearing tee shirt and shorts, and carrying a clipboard with notes, he talks with village chiefs and checks progress on rural projects initiated by him and the Queen.

In 1979, a year after I became IAUP President-Elect, Ginny and I first met the King, whose two avocations are philosophy and jazz. The meeting was arranged by a mutual friend, Nibondh Sasidhorn, who, with some exaggeration, told His Majesty that I was an "expert on Plato." At the Summer Palace where we were visiting, the King entered the room, closely followed by two grim-faced and beribboned generals. With his nose only a few inches from mine, he said, "I understand you are an expert on Plato." "Well, not really, Sir," I replied. At this the King scowled and said, "You wrote a book on Plato, didn't you?" When I answered affirmatively, his eyes narrowed and he snapped, "Okay then, you're an expert!" I thought about this for a few seconds, and then wisely decided not to argue further. I had twice seen *The King and I* on Broadway, and remembered what happened to people who angered Yul Brynner.

Because of his modesty and good works, the King is revered by his people. This became clear five years later, in 1984, in a hotel lobby in Bangkok, at the outset of the VII IAUP Triennial Conference. Ginny and I were once again lined up with others to greet the King. When he reached Ginny he said, pointing to me, "Does he know anything more about Plato than he did five years ago?" He was so delighted with this comment that he tapped me playfully on the arm. So I playfully tapped him back. Whereupon several courtiers turned white. An agitated Nibondh rushed to my side and whispered, "Never touch King!" "Why not?" I asked. "He touched me." "Not same thing," Nibondh replied, "You not King."

In 1978, one year before I first met the King of Thailand, I encountered his opposite—the Shah of Iran. My first assignment as the new President-Elect of IAUP was to organize 200 presidents for a reception to be given by their Majesties in the gardens of the Imperial Palace, on the occasion of the organization's fifth Triennial Conference. My assistant for this task was Manouchehr Ganji, Minister of Education. As ordered by the Shah, we attempted, with limited success, to arrange the presidents in a straight line, alphabetically by country. Some presidents, mindful of their high status, refused to be "pushed around." The whole scene reminded me of trying to get the faculty lined up for the annual commencement ceremony.

After going through the reception line, the Shah suddenly got stuck with some guests, a common problem for hosts everywhere. Minister Ganji was annoyed. "Go tell him to move around," he whispered. "Who me?" I whispered back incredulously. "Why don't *you* tell him?" I lost the argument, went over to the Shah, and said timidly, "Your Majesty, Minister Ganji and I think it would be helpful if you moved around." He stared at me as if I were an ant, frowned scornfully, and held his ground. But five minutes later I noted, from the corner of my eye, that he had begun to move around, though not happily.

Unlike the King of Thailand, the Shah was a haughty and ultimately insecure leader. To be sure, he industrialized Iran, and he advanced the status of women. Under the Shah, and thanks to the subtle influence of Empress Farah, women constituted almost 50 percent of university students, and were fully integrated with males in the classroom. No more curtains down the middle of the room. But he typically associated with diplomats, business executives, and his own ministers and generals. He made no effort to "get down" with the people, who a few months later blew him away in an Islamic revolution. By contrast, in fifty years there has never been a coup against the King of Thailand. Neither the people nor the army would ever permit it.

Some of Snow's leaders communicated by example, some by listening, and some by getting down among the people. But others communicated by metaphor, analogy, symbol, and other figures of speech. The most prominent here was Robert Frost, whose poetry readings attracted ordinary people from hundreds of miles away. Frost was after all a poet, and we would expect him to speak in figures of speech. But, in fact, most leaders are poets by nature. Most instinctively speak in metaphor, personification, and other figures. In his autobiography, Charles de Gaulle tells of addressing paratroopers during a period of military revolt in Algeria (then a French colony) and civil strife at home. Tears streamed down the toughened troopers' faces when he described France as a "tattered old lady" in urgent need of rescue. Figures of speech carry great emotional power.

Some leaders have used symbols as part of their body language. King Alfred led his warriors into battle holding a sword in front of him like a cross. Peter the Great wore peasant's boots to identify with the masses. For the same reason, Bellaunde Terry, an intellectual who became President of Peru, sprinkled talcum powder on his shoulders. The powder resembled dandruff, and showed that he too was a common man at heart.

Of all the leaders Snow describes in *Varieties of Men*, the most humorous to him was Winston Churchill. But Churchill was really witty, not humorous. Humor is warm, self-directed, and makes friends. Wit is cold, other-directed, and often makes enemies. Churchill not only made enemies through his wit, but reveled in doing so. At a dinner party, a British dowager once said to him, "Sir Winston, you are drunk." He replied, "You are correct, madam. I am drunk and you are ugly. But there is a difference between us. I shall be sober tomorrow."

In terms of communication as the chief vehicle of style, the most unusual leader I ever worked with was Albert Parker, founding president of Hanover College in Indiana (see Chapters 13 and 16). Parker communicated (and achieved his objectives) by silence. He said almost nothing at any time, and to my best knowledge, never wrote anything down. He was kin to the Catholic nuns who once visited a modern church in Valparaiso, Indiana, at the same time Ginny and I did. They were obviously distraught at the bizarre architecture. When they reached the Visitor's Book at the end of the tour, they whispered among themselves for a minute or so, then one of them hurriedly wrote something down. As Ginny and I stepped up to sign the book, we could see what the nun had written. Under the "Comments" column was scribbled, almost illegibly, "No comment."

Parker was a perpetual "no comment" man. To deflect unwanted dialogue, he was not above balancing an eighteen inch ruler on his bald head, or conspicuously wiping his Parker (no relation) pen on his socks. On one occasion in my presence, he studiously constructed a slingshot from a pencil and a rubber band, then sped a paper clip toward a wall painting he disliked. When during the same session I made the mistake of placing my hands on his bare glass desktop, he quickly took out his handkerchief and wiped off the smudges.

Parker's tactics always mesmerized his visitors, who immediately forgot what they had come to talk about. His strange actions were never accompanied by any comment except an occasional "Oh?" or "Ah!" By these primitive expressions he deliberately created conversational voids into which others ventured to their own destruction. If a businessman said he could not give a gift, Parker would say "Oh?" If the man got nervous and said, "Well, what about $10,000?" Parker would say "Ah!" He was simply a genius at saying nothing. Yet by any measurement you want to choose, he was an extraordinarily successful college president.

As noted earlier, leadership style is largely an unconscious mixture of birth, temperament, experience, study, occupation, and luck. Of these ingredients, the most important for Alfred North Whitehead, in *Aims of Education*, was one's occupation and the academic studies leading to it. I never thought much about Whitehead's view until forced to do so. Some years back, Columbia University's Graduate School of Business invited me to speak on the relationship of my humanities background to my alleged leadership style. In preparing for the lecture, I realized for the first time that the humanities had deeply affected the way I operated administratively, for better or worse.

More specifically, I discovered that my leadership style had been much influenced by my studying, teaching and writing of poetry, history, and philosophy during my student and professional years. In contrast to prose, poetry is characterized by compression, structure, and rhythm. In my early administrative life, compression was a problem for me. But I gradually discovered that in communication, acorns are preferable to oaks. Short memos, or preferably face-to-face discussions, are far more effective than complex documents and argumentative "broadsides." As for structure, a poem has no meaning without it, regardless of whether the structure is a sonnet or the free verse of William Carlos Williams. Likewise, no leader can accomplish his objectives without structure. Nothing can be accomplished unless the right people cooperate with each other within an effective table of organization. The Boston Red Sox once had "a star at every position," but the team lost more games than it won because the stars were not working together. They were talented beyond words, but they played like nine one-man teams, rather than one nine-man organization.

As for poetic rhythm, it might seem to be irrelevant for leadership, but in fact leadership is nothing without the "rhythm" of timing. Seasonally speaking, the best time to introduce a new idea to faculty is spring, when the sun finally breaks through the clouds, the crocuses pop their jaunty heads through the thinning snow, and everyone is happy and upbeat at winter's retreat. My informal data suggests that the faculty's acceptance/rejection ratio is about five to one in spring. This ratio goes up to about seven to one if the new idea is labeled as "strictly experimental," or "subject to later review."

Outstanding ideas often fail if voted upon too early or too late in a faculty meeting. If friends can be found, the time to have them propose the vote is when the momentum of discussion is *toward* the proposal, especially if *Roberts' Rules of Order* can be used to one's advantage at that moment. My most disastrous experience with Roberts was during my first meeting as a college dean. I had distributed a specific agenda, which apparently alarmed the faculty. After my call to order, a tall mathematics professor immediately jumped up and shouted, "I move we adjourn." His crony, a short sociologist, seconded the motion. "This is crazy!" I said. "We haven't even begun. Please sit down." At that point William Allen, a history professor who had long been the college parliamentarian, rushed forward and whispered in my ear, "If a motion to adjourn is made and seconded, there can be no debate. It must immediately be voted upon." "Says who?" I asked indignantly. "Says Roberts," he said. So I called the vote. More than the necessary two-thirds were hugely in favor, so everyone scrambled out of the room, leaving me alone and forlorn with the parliamentarian. His "Sorry" was belied by his sly smile as he showed me the relevant page from Roberts' *Rules of Order.*

My history research in the Renaissance also influenced my ideas of leadership. Some of my research was on Sir (later Saint) Thomas More, who at least in his early life not only tolerated rival views, but sought cautiously to reconcile Christian and pagan philosophy. This moderated tolerance is a central doctrine of Chapter 13 on "Open Minds." During the writing of this book, I have also referred to Machiavelli and *The Prince* more than once. Early in this century he was reviled as a philosopher who taught that good ends justify evil means. This interpretation now seems to me, and to many other scholars, to be far too simplistic. What appears to be an evil end is often the lesser of two evils. When Truman authorized the nuclear bombing of Hiroshima to end World War II, he described it as the best evil possible. The greater evil, he argued, would have been to invade Japan, a choice which, as he saw it, would have killed far more people on both sides.

Leaders frequently find themselves in Truman's place. They need to choose among options, none of which is palatable. Do we release 20 percent of the faculty and staff, or do we let the institution collapse? A decision here might not be as important for the world as Hiroshima, but the principle underlying the decision is the same. In Jeremy Bentham's phrase, we try under such circumstances to achieve "the greatest good for the greatest number."

During the Renaissance, of which More and Machiavelli were a part, the chief doctrine was perfectibility, the notion that anything was possible. There never has been a more optimistic period in human endeavor. In the *Dignity of Man*, the Italian humanist Pico Della Mirandola even argued that man was at the center of the universe. Through free will, he could merge mystically with the deity, or even become God. During an especially dark day at UB, when my financial vice president, Harry Rowell, and I were trying desperately to balance the budget, he suddenly swiveled around in his chair and exclaimed, "Where do you get your optimism?" Having given the lecture at Columbia University, I now know the answer—the Renaissance gave it to me.

Optimism, in my judgment, is the indispensable quality of a leader. The multitude of everyday problems can make the administrator's life intolerable unless there's some ideal beyond the daily battle. In Plato's system, there are two worlds—that of being, and that of becoming. The latter, in which you and I live, is always striving toward the former. It's a good system for leaders to believe in. It's a system where one's success comes largely from striving, not achieving—a point frequently made in earlier chapters of this book, sometimes by reference to Robert Browning.

In many ways, Plato has been my intellectual father. I first "met" him as a Juniata senior when I took a one-person honors course from Calvert Ellis, the college president. Each week I would come to his office, and we would talk about the *Apology* or *Crito* or *Phaedo* or some other glorious dialogue in which Socrates played dumb. By asking "innocent" questions, he was always maneuvering opponents into humorously indefensible positions. I realize now that Plato's Scale of Values, which figures prominently in Chapters 11 and 13 of this book, is at the root of my emphasis on prioritizing, not just ethically, but corporately. It seems to me impossible to lead if one does not have a set of priorities, not just for himself but for his followers. That's why I believe in "management by (mutually developed) objectives," or MBO, and long range (now called strategic) planning. These techniques compel leaders and their associates to sort out priorities, to determine where they're headed, no matter how much they might tack later on. Some critics say that it is dangerous to plan because we cannot predict the future. But I say it is even more dangerous to drift without a rudder.

No doubt my early work with poetry, history, and philosophy influenced my later leadership style. But an even greater influence was drama, as taught and practiced by an extraordinary woman. Possibly the most important event in my life was coming to Juniata College on a drama scholarship in 1941, to be student assistant to a new theater director named Esther Doyle, and to learn about theater in Oller Hall, which was then brand new. Esther believed that one learned by doing, so she immediately appointed me as the "Lighting Artist," even though at that point I did not know the difference between a male and female plug. She also made me stage manager for *Pinafore* and other operettas, even though I kept stumbling over the flat braces while warning the stage crew to be quiet.

My favorite Doyle appointment was as rehearsal actor – that is, as the actor who played various parts opposite the students who were auditioning for *Stage Door* or whatever. Esther also cast me, at the age of 19, as Grandpa in *You Can't Take It With You*, a role I have gradually evolved into over time. At her insistence, I also played Jabez Stone, who sells his soul to Mr. Scratch, the Devil, in Stephen Vincent Benet's *The Devil and Daniel Webster.* The Benet play was the only time Esther and I almost had a falling out. I did not want to play Stone; I was hell-bent to play the Devil. She resisted, but I was later vindicated. As a university president, many faculty members saw me as Mr. Scratch in disguise.

For many years after I left Juniata, I felt guilty at not going into the theatre. I feared I had let Esther down. After all, I had written an emotional essay at Juniata, contending that I would, if necessary, be a janitor sweeping theater floors. But gradually I have realized that Shakespeare was right—all the world is indeed a stage. Drama is not only *As You Like It*; it exists everywhere. The best professors, lecturers, and leaders of all types are "dramatic" – that is, they have an instinct for timing, a gift for speaking, a knack for humor, a compassion for others, an ingenuity in crises, and a capacity to work cheerfully and constructively with many kinds of real-life characters. All this Esther subtly taught me, through the example of her own vibrant personality, even though I wasn't aware of it at the time, and have not always lived up to it since.

For me, the humanities have had the biggest impact on my leadership style. But all disciplines, from poetry to physics, from anthropology to mathematics, are relevant to leadership. All help to develop qualities of mind which can, and often do, produce distinctive leadership styles, which for Whitehead are the source of power. As I look back on more than a quarter of a century in university administration, it seems to me that leadership, especially in universities, withers if cut off from its scholarly roots. When that happens, it loses its vibrancy and integrity, and becomes sadly mechanical. The fortunate leader is one who, day in and day out, remains conscious of his academic past, and draws on it for spiritual and intellectual sustenance. This kind of leader will be more effective, more powerful if you will, and certainly more wise, than the one who forgets his roots and begins just to go through the administrative routines.

Students who in their later years find themselves in leadership positions should remember that any leadership position is temporary. At the top of the pyramid, it is lonely, windy and slippery, and there are always those who are ready to give you a shove from the tier below. In the Middle Ages, there was a legend about the Goddess Fortune, who spun a Wheel onto which leaders climbed. When Fortune capriciously turned the Wheel, those leaders who were on top went down, and vice versa.

Despite the essential truth of this Fortune motif, most leaders take themselves too seriously. Periodically they need to be pulled down a peg or two. For me, this function was performed by program chairmen as I moved around the lecture circuit. Take for example the weary no-nonsense high school superintendent in Ohio who introduced me as follows: "Some people say this fellow can talk. Some say he can't. Let's see." What a send-off! I was so unnerved as I approached the lectern that I stumbled over the one flowerpot on the stage and almost pitched headfirst into the orchestra pit. My best introduction (up to a point) was at Centre College in Danville, Kentucky. Here the chairman began by saying, "Not everyone can be a paragon of the intellect" and wound up several minutes later by roaring, "and not everyone can be in the avant garde of the liberal educators of the land." He then paused, smiled at the audience, and said, "But enough of myself. Now for a few words about our speaker."

But let's come back to commencements. Are commencement speakers trying to flatter the audience, or do colleges really produce leaders? I never read a college catalogue that didn't make that claim. All I know for sure is that if students take away from their college experience the qualities of mind discussed in this book, they will be prepared to live creatively, to work honestly, to follow intelligently, and to function responsibly as citizens. Are these qualities also the ones which will guarantee leadership? Definitely not. As already noted, becoming a leader depends on many factors, including luck. According to some scholars, Napoleon lost at Waterloo because he had hemorrhoids, and could not mount his horse that day. The qualities which students can take from college, if their alma maters have given them a modern education, will prepare them to lead if the opportunity arises. If it does not, they will at least have the satisfaction of knowing they were ready.

Epilogue

WHEN I BECAME president of Alfred University, the first piece of paper to cross my desk was a letter from the National League for Nursing, rejecting Alfred's request for national accreditation in that field. The letter came as a shock, because Alfred's nursing graduates were widely admired. They spent their middle two years off campus at Rochester hospitals, being superbly trained in maternal/child health, psychological, and community nursing. That experience, together with their first and fourth years on campus taking liberal arts courses, produced young women who were competent, caring, and broad-minded. The most delightful students in any Alfred crowd were senior nursing majors.

So what was the problem? When I visited NLN headquarters in New York, I soon found out. The accrediting agency was not interested in the *quality* of the nursing graduates. Their concern was with the *structure* of the curriculum. "You have a one-two-one," they explained, in typical NLN jargon. "We require a two-two structure." Translated, that meant that Alfred's nursing program could not gain accreditation unless all the liberal arts courses were placed in the first two years, with the remaining time devoted to clinical nursing.

This emphasis on process rather than product is typical of most accrediting bodies. Their interest is in how many Ph.D.'s are on the faculty, how many volumes are in the library, how many computers are available to students, how many full-time faculty are teaching as distinguished from part-time instructors. The American Assembly for Schools and Colleges of Business (AASCB) limits the percentage of part-time teachers, thus depriving many business colleges of the opportunity to use Fortune 500 executives as adjunct professors. Yet such corporate leaders are the most exciting kind of instructor for business students, because they use their own companies as "case studies" rather than merely discussing the theory of management.

In this book I have sought to stress product, not process. To be sure, I have made many "process" suggestions along the way, most of them hopefully more rational than the NLN's. But my emphasis has been on the skills and qualities that colleges should develop in students, regardless of how they achieve those ends. I have argued that colleges should produce students who have mastered the basics and become competent in their chosen fields, yet are knowledgeable and appreciative of the many other areas of human endeavor. If a college has done its job, graduates will take risks, see failure as part of learning, and communicate with ease and grace before any kind of audience. They will be comfortable with divergent ideas, seek to learn more beyond college, and recognize the value of non-conformity, especially when based on conscience. They will be able to strike a balance between intellect and emotion, understand the importance and nature of friendship, and like or love people for their characters, not for what they look like or wear.

Any college would be rightly proud to produce such students. But I am asking for more. Anyone who graduates from college should have learned to respect the great works of the past, yet be able to adjust to the acceleration of change that categorizes the New Millennium. Critical to success in the modern world, graduates should have learned to open their minds, respect contrary views, and hold to principles with the understanding that, being human, they might someday be persuaded otherwise. Especially as we move into the 21st Century, colleges should produce graduates who are sensitive to the issues raised by modern technology, to the need to protect the earth while it is still habitable, and to the importance of cross-cultural understanding in an increasingly interdependent world. As possible future leaders, such students should have the opportunity to learn how followers shape leaders, the sources of various leadership styles, and the proper aim of leading—not to advance oneself, but to inspire others to work toward a just society.

The above represents my idea of what a college education should be, as we move past 2000 A.D. Admittedly, no college can achieve all the goals put forward here. That's where lifetime learning comes in. But depending on the temperament and background of each student, many of these goals can be achieved if a college organizes itself to do so. If I were asked to accredit a given college, I would focus on the *product*, that is, the extent to which the alumni ten or twenty years out from graduation matched my profile of an educated person. Through research, questionnaires, and selective interviewing, I would seek answers to such questions as: What are you doing now in work and play? What is your scale of values? How has your thinking and behavior been influenced by your alma mater? Who are your friends and why? What are your contributions to the community? Do you have long-term goals for career and family? If so, what are they?

Some will say that this approach is terribly impractical. I can concede that the current method of accreditation *is* practical, but it is also irrelevant. The same applies to the "Best Colleges" ratings of magazines like *U.S. News & World Report*, which allows only 5 percent of its rating to apply to alumni. Even then, the 5 percent is confined to alumni giving, not alumni quality as individuals and professionals. Large libraries, sophisticated equipment, many Ph.D.'s and elite status do not guarantee that a college will produce "successful" students, either in salary, position, character, or community service. Harvard has produced its share of Supreme Court justices, but among its graduates have been some at the opposite pole.

Listen to Professor Andrew Hacker, a professor of political science at Queens College of the City University of New York. His latest book is entitled *Money: Who Has How Much, and Why?* Despite the title, much of this book examines higher education. Americans cannot get by without a bachelor's degree, Dr. Hacker writes. But contrary to what high school guidance counselors say, it is largely irrelevant which institution grants the degree. "Once you get the B.A.," Hacker argues, "it can be from Texas Tech or St. Olaf, and within a short period of time that's good enough." As an example, he points out that of the 100 chief executives of the country's largest corporations and financial firms, only 11 received their undergraduate degrees from Ivy League schools. Much more prominent among the group were graduates from institutions like Tennessee Tech and North Carolina State. "When we look at the graduates of selective colleges, say thirty years later, the results are disappointing," Hacker writes. "Few have carved out distinctive careers."

Of course, the aim of college should be to produce distinctive persons, not distinctive careers—persons who are interesting, inspiring, and stimulating in addition to being (as Hacker says elsewhere) "good providers and responsible citizens." The colleges least likely to produce such people are those that train for jobs only, and those at the other end which play ostrich by ignoring the world of work. At one extreme are the "proprietary" or for-profit schools like the Culinary Institute of America, and at the other, the wholly liberal arts colleges which overlook the fact that most students must earn a livelihood after graduation. Conversely, the colleges most likely to produce the type of graduate described herein are those which provide professional training within a liberal arts atmosphere, regardless of whether the institutions are public or private, selective or non-selective, big or small.

The great advantage of such institutions is that they avoid excessive specialization, which has been a chief plague of the 20th Century. This plague has affected all our activities, even sports. A religious friend of mine was recently on an airliner where half of the seats were occupied by the Notre Dame football team, their coaches, and assorted staff. My friend was pleased to find himself seated next to the team's co-captain. "Tell me," he said to the player, "What goes on when all of you huddle on the sideline just before the game?" "Oh, we just pray together with our chaplains," replied the player, pointing to two men in clerical garb seated separately some rows back. "That's wonderful," said my friend. "Could I meet one of them?" "Sure," responded the co-captain. "Which one would you like to meet—the offensive or the defensive chaplain?"

Regardless of what kind of college a student attends in the future, technology will play an important role, but not so important as certain extravagant claims would suggest. For example, the April '97 issue of the *Royal Society of Arts Journal* features an article by Sir Geoffrey Holland, head of the University of Exeter. "The young people of today," he writes, "are the first generation in history to have accessible on demand the entire heritage of human knowledge." To say that Sir Geoffrey overstates would be an understatement. In Chapter 3 of this book, I noted that the Internet had been oversold as a teaching and research tool. This conclusion is endorsed by Edward Rothstein, editor of the Technology section of the *New York Times*, in a July 7, 1997, article. His article is accompanied by a cartoon showing a computer-like robot crashing through library bookshelves, scattering books in all directions. That won't happen very soon, Rothstein says, and continues, "The Internet will not come close to replacing even the most ordinary library until every book of importance is published in digital form, financial arrangements are worked out with publishers, and search engines become as powerful as the index in back of a reference book. Right now, even the most limited local library has much the Internet cannot touch."

All of this is by way of saying that technology notwithstanding, books and teachers will continue to be at the center of college education for a long time. I spent Chapter 10 defining great books; let me now attempt to sketch the profile of a great teacher. Michael Porte, a professor of communication at the University of Cincinnati, once sent me a single sheet of paper, on which he sought to distinguish between a "good" teacher and a "great" one. In essence he wrote that great teachers are not only informed but passionate. They not only lecture but listen. They not only prepare students for exams, but inspire them to seek knowledge. They have an ethical code, but also manifest it in their behavior and decisions. They warn students of the pitfalls ahead, but also urge them to take risks and grow. They teach students how to think critically, but also how to love. They train students for professions, but also urge them to let their imaginations be enhanced by the arts and humanities.

To this thoughtful description of great teachers, I would add only one point. Great teachers excite students by showing them the relevance of their subjects to their everyday lives and the modern issues they will face. The "Bower of Bliss" in Edmund Spenser's 16th Century *Fairy Queen* is only the forerunner of the temptations that seduce and corrupt modern leaders. Similarly, the 15th Century Spanish Inquisition foreshadows an array of later terrorist activities, including the Salem witchcraft trials in early America, and the religiously-inspired "ethnic cleansing" in what was once Yugoslavia. Knowledge is, of course, valuable for its own sake, as mentioned earlier (Chapter 12). But students are drawn to it more readily if they can see the connection to their own lives and concerns.

Showing the relevance of a subject often requires translating theory into practice. A recent example here is the Center for Undergraduate Philosophical Analysis, founded at Trinity University in San

Antonio in 1989. The philosophy majors selected to work in this laboratory are divided into three teams. The "Logical Detectives" take on such projects as exploring a real life treasure hunt that began two hundred years ago in Nova Scotia. Students must evaluate the relative plausibility of each of the theories as to what is buried there. The second group, the "Disaster Team," examines the moral ramifications of U.S. crises, specifically AIDS and drug epidemics. In the latter instance, a student plays the role of a national drug czar, who questions various advisors and then recommends how to proceed. The third team, the "Conceptual Cartographers" develops computerized teaching materials on governmental issues for high school students.

What do all these projects have to do with philosophy? That is a question frequently asked of Peter French, the department chairman and founder of the Center. His answer is "a lot." By applying theory to real life situations, he says, students are practicing such skills as logic, critical reasoning, and the application of moral responsibility in decision making—skills that national studies have shown to be sorely lacking among many of today's college students. "When I told my parents I was going to be a philosophy major, I thought they would drop dead," said Nancy Adams, captain of the AIDS Disaster Team. "But in this lab, we're learning how our classroom discussions apply to real-world problems."

Like books and teachers, parents' influence, for better or worse, will continue to be an important factor in education. Michael Porte's profile of a great teacher can easily be adapted to parents. "Great" parents are passionate about knowledge, listen and learn from their children, inspire them to be curious, exemplify ethical behavior, challenge children to grow, insist that they think critically, and teach them to love. Among the many parents I have met over the years, some have measured up to this profile. Others have despaired of their children's ability to do anything significant. They anticipate that their offspring will fail in college, and are prepared to sell them short. But young people who seem ordinary often wind up doing extraordinary things. My friend Mike Balzano was a high school dropout and garbage collector. By a sheer act of will, he suddenly pulled up his socks and went on to graduate from UB, get a Ph.D. from Georgetown University, write a book, and become director of the American Enterprise Institute.

I'm not Balzano, but I did have my own problems in starting off on the right foot. By the time I was twelve, I had already pushed my brother off the roof (the house was only one story high); hidden "Rover," our Chesapeake Retriever, when a couple came to buy him from my father; been kicked out of the Methodist Sunday School for throwing spit-balls; and run away after provisioning myself with bubble gum at Shapiro's Drug Store. Even as a teenager, I was a problem, especially with the family car. It seemed that no matter where I parked, some wall would move up and dent a fender. The morning following one such occasion, my father asked where I had been. "Just out with the fellows," I said. "Okay," he replied. "Next time you see 'em, tell 'em I found one of their lipsticks in the back seat." Later in life, if this book is an honest document, I managed to redeem myself. It was the kind of meta-morphosis that occurs in most families, if parents are patient enough. College can be a major factor in effecting that change. It was for me.

Biographical Note

On one level, Provoking Thought *is a non-chronological memoir. During the book's market tests, some readers expressed the need for a chronological summary to which they could refer on occasion. Hence this biographical note.*

Leland Miles' college career at Juniata College in Pennsylvania was interrupted by World War II. As a twenty-year-old navigator in China for Chennault's Flying Tigers, he twice won the Distinguished Flying Cross. After returning to Juniata for his undergraduate degree, he earned a multi-disciplinary Ph.D. at the University of North Carolina at Chapel Hill in 1949, with the help of recent bride Virginia and the GI Bill.

As a Fulbright and American Council of Learned Societies scholar at the University of London and Harvard, he became an authority on Plato and St. Thomas More, and for many years co-edited a series of books on British history and culture published by the New York University Press. He also served as Contributing Editor of National Forum, *the journal of the academic honor society Phi Kappa Phi.*

Parallel with these scholarly activities (1950's through '70's), the author produced and moderated "Casing the Classics," a popular television program over WHAS-TV in Louisville and other CBS stations. While a professor at Hanover College in Indiana and the University of Cincinnati, he was also a favorite "repeater" on the national lecture circuit, treating humorously the classics, philosophy, and American life. At Hanover daughter Christine, son Gregory, and dog Beowulf joined the Miles family. He first met many of his future business friends at the Aspen Institute in Colorado, where he moderated executive seminars on great books.

As an author, Dr. Miles is known for the versatility of his writings, which have appeared in both learned journals and popular magazines, e.g., The New York Times, Vital Speeches of the Day, International Herald Tribune, The Rotarian, American Society of Engineering Education Journal, *and* Studies in the Renaissance. *On one occasion, two of his articles appeared simultaneously in the* Anglican Theological Review *and the* San Quentin Prison News.

Over twenty years (1970's and '80's), Dr. Miles served as president of two institutions, Alfred University in New York, and the University of Bridgeport in Connecticut, where he founded the Law School and Centers on Aging and Venture Management. He has chaired or served as a member of many corporate, non-profit, foundation, and consortia boards, including Grolier, Inc., the Empire State Foundation, Save the Children, English Speaking Union, Forum for World Affairs, United Illuminating, Western New York Nuclear Research Center, Academic Collective Bargaining Information Service, College Center of the Finger Lakes,

169

Connecticut Grand Opera, and the Ettinger Scholarship Program for the Educational Foundation of America.

As a university president, Dr. Miles was on the cutting edge of higher education, gaining recognition for his creativity, innovative spirit, and bold proposals. Something of a maverick, he was not one to dodge debate. He denounced the National League for Nursing for their accreditation process, proposed that Connecticut subsidize private colleges, opened a dialogue with Polish academics while Poland was still Communist, supported and introduced ROTC programs when they were unpopular, and urged liberal arts faculty to serve professional students rather than wringing their hands at the loss of humanities majors. During the now famous "student unrest" period (1967-1974), he was the only American college president to take a case of student disruption to a high court, and win. The incident became a moot court case in the nation's law schools.

In recent years, the author entered a new career phase as a leader in international education. His 1982 Boston speech on "Universities for Peace" was widely reprinted, praised, and distributed both here and abroad. As a recent president of the International Association of University Presidents, he has been honored by the French, Chinese, and pre-revolutionary Iranian governments for his contributions to international understanding.

From 1991 to 1996, Dr. Miles founded and chaired the IAUP/UN Commission on Disarmament Education, Conflict Resolution, and Peace, which introduced peace curricula into seventy universities in the Third World. He is the author of five books, and has contributed chapters to many others, including Great Political Thinkers *(London 1995),* War and Public Health *(Oxford University Press, 1997), and* The Cultural Miracle of America *(1999). In 1996, the United Nations published his report on "Disarmament Education in Africa." He is a Life Fellow of the Royal Society of Arts, Manufactures, and Commerce in London.*

Provoking
Thought

has been published in a first edition
of fifteen hundred copies.
Designed by A. L. Morris,
the text was composed in Garamond Light
and printed by J. S. McCarthy / Letter Systems
in Augusta, Maine on Cougar Opaque Natural.
The jacket was printed on Potlach Vintage Velvet,
and the binding in ICG Holliston Arrestox
and Rainbow Colonial
was executed by New Hampshire Bindery
in Concord, New Hampshire.